THE BEST OF **Good Housekeeping**

LIGHT & EASY

THE BEST OF **Good Housekeeping**
LIGHT & EASY

Over 175 delicious, low-calorie recipes

LONDON   NEW YORK   SYDNEY   TORONTO

First published 1996

1 3 5 7 9 10 8 6 4 2

This edition published by BCA in 1996 by arrangement with Ebury Press, Random House,
20 Vauxhall Bridge Road, London SW1V 2SA

Cookery Notes
- Both metric and imperial measures are given for the recipes. Follow either metric or imperial
throughout as they are not interchangeable.
- All spoon measures are level unless otherwise stated. Sets of measuring spoons are
available in metric and imperial for accurate measurement of small quantities.
- Ovens should be preheated to the specified temperature. Grills should also be preheated.
The cooking times given in the recipes assume that this has been done.
- Size 2 eggs should be used except where otherwise specified. Free-range eggs are
recommended.
- Use fresh rather than dried herbs unless dried herbs are suggested in the recipe.

CN 2069

Editor: Vicky Hanson
Design: Christine Wood

Printed in Singapore by Tien Wah Press

CONTENTS

INTRODUCTION

You don't have to compromise on taste and settle for bland, uninspiring food just because you are watching the calories. Food can be every bit as tempting and full of flavour whether you are trying to lose weight or are just keen to maintain a healthy diet – the recipes in this book are proof of that. Every one contains no more than 350 calories yet there are original and delicious ideas which are sure to tempt the most discriminating of palates. We've also made sure that there is a wide variety of recipes for all kinds of different occasions, including quick suppers, family meals and more special dishes for entertaining, so that you never have to feel forced into cooking more fattening food simply because you are short of time or want to present special guests with something elaborate.

In addition to the recipes you choose, there are, of course, other ways in which you can cut down the calories in your cooking. The cooking method is important - frying food in a large amount of fat will obviously add calories whereas the cooking methods described below are much more beneficial.

GRILLING

Grilling is an excellent way of cooking meat, fish, poultry and some vegetables. It requires little or no fat to be added during cooking. Grilling is ideal for cooking tender, even-sized cuts of meat which are not too thick. It's not suitable for tough cuts of meat as the intense heat will toughen the texture of the fibres even more. Grilling is a good method for cooking oily fish such as mackerel and herrings, but take care when grilling delicate white fish, as they can dry out quickly. Vegetables such as mushrooms, courgettes, peppers, aubergines and tomatoes can be grilled successfully; brush them with a little oil first.

STIR-FRYING

Stir-fried food has a good texture and flavour. It's a quick method of cooking and this helps to preserve vitamins as well as flavour. Much less fat is required than for shallow-frying. Make sure that all the vegetables are cut into similar-size pieces so that they cook quickly in the same amount of time. Use a wok or deep-sided frying pan and ensure that the oil is really hot before you add the ingredients.

ROASTING

This is a healthy way of cooking meat and poultry. Place the joint or bird on a rack over a roasting tin so that the fat drips underneath and remove any fat before using the remaining juices. Roasting is also an excellent way of cooking certain vegetables, such as courgettes, aubergines, onions, garlic and peppers, especially if they are cut into chunks and blanched in boiling water first.

STEAMING

Steaming is one of the best methods for cooking vegetables and one which requires no added fat. It helps to retain their flavour, colour and the water-soluble vitamins which are easily lost during other cooking methods. Some other foods, such as fish and grains, can also be steamed.

BOILING

Boiling requires no added fat. However, the water-soluble vitamins present in vegetables can easily be lost during cooking. To help preserve these vitamins, add the vegetables to a small amount of boiling water and cook for as short a time as possible, until they are just tender but retain some 'bite'.

As well as the basic cooking method, there are other tricks for saving on calories. Below are some hints.

10 WAYS TO SAVE 100 CALORIES

1 Add dressing to salads sparingly. 15 ml (1 tbsp) French dressing = 100 calories

2 Remove the skin from chicken before eating (although you should generally leave it on during cooking to keep it moist, unless otherwise specified in the recipe).
150 g (5 oz) chicken breast without skin = 182 calories
150 g (5 oz) chicken breast with skin = 345 calories

3 Don't nibble with drinks - even a small handful of nibbles can have a lot of calories.
Small handful (25 g/1 oz) peanuts = 141 calories

Small amount of crisps (25 g/1 oz) = 153 calories

4 Serve Greek yogurt rather than cream to accompany desserts.
30 g (1 tbsp) double cream = 135 calories
45 g (1 tbsp) low-fat Greek yogurt = 36 calories

5 Cut out sugar in tea and coffee. 5 ml (1 level tsp) sugar contains 16 calories, so 6 cups of tea or coffee per day adds up to almost 100 calories from sugar alone.

6 Choose 'diet' fizzy drinks.
1 can cola drink (330 ml) = 129 calories
1 can diet cola (330 ml) = 0 calories

7 To minimize the amount of oil needed when softening vegetables etc, use a heavy-based, nonstick pan. Oil expands when it gets hot, so you don't need to add as much as you think.
15 ml (1 tbsp) vegetable oil = 117 calories

8 Use skimmed or semi-skimmed milk.
500 ml (1 pint) full cream milk = 364 calories
500 ml (1 pint) semi-skimmed milk = 252 calories
500 ml (1 pint) skimmed milk = 184 calories

9 Choose reduced-fat alternatives when available. Lasagne made with skimmed milk, reduced-fat cheese and lean mince, for example = 430 calories per serving. The same recipe made with full-fat ingredients = 570 calories.

10 Keep a choice of low-calorie snacks on hand, so that more fattening choices such as biscuits don't tempt you.
1 apple = 47 calories
4 prunes = 56 calories
small banana = 120 calories
1 average chocolate bar = 250 calories

SOUPS, STARTERS & LIGHT MEALS

CHICKEN AND MANGO SALAD

Preparation time: 10–15 minutes
Cooking time: nil

SERVES 6

This is delicious as a starter, or you can double the quantities and serve it for a main course.

25 g (1 oz) toasted hazelnuts
75 ml (3 fl oz) low-calorie salad dressing
75 ml (3 fl oz) fresh orange juice
a handful of rocket or watercress sprigs, chopped
350 g (12 oz) cold roast chicken or smoked sliced duck, skinned
2 little gem lettuce hearts, or red or green endive
1 ripe mango
rocket and watercress, to garnish

1 Roughly chop the nuts. Whisk together with the salad dressing, orange juice and chopped rocket or watercress sprigs.
2 Thinly slice the chicken. Slice the lettuce hearts, if using, or separate the leaves of the endive.
3 Peel and thinly slice the mango.
4 Arrange the lettuce on individual plates. Add a few slices of mango. Top with slices of chicken or duck. Spoon over a little dressing and garnish with rocket or watercress.

NOT SUITABLE FOR FREEZING
215 Calories per serving

WARM SEAFOOD SALAD WITH TOASTED POLENTA

Preparation time: 15 minutes
Cooking time: 15 minutes

SERVES 6

75 g (3 oz) polenta
150 ml (¼ pint) low-calorie salad dressing
1 garlic clove, skinned and crushed
30 ml (2 tbsp) chopped fresh herbs, eg thyme, chives, parsley
350 g (12 oz) smoked haddock fillet
175 g (6 oz) cooked, peeled prawns

1 Make up the polenta according to packet instructions. Spoon on to a sheet of foil, cool slightly, then press into a rectangle about 1 cm (½ inch) thick. Leave to cool.
2 Whisk together the dressing, garlic and half of the herbs. Thinly slice the haddock. Place the fish and prawns in a single layer in a shallow, flameproof dish. Pour over the dressing. Cover and refrigerate.
3 Cut the cooled polenta into 7.5 cm (3 inch) triangles. Grill for about 4 minutes on each side until golden.
4 Remove the fish and prawns from the dressing and grill for 1–2 minutes, basting with the dressing. Serve the polenta with the warm fish and prawns, sprinkled with the remaining herbs.

NOT SUITABLE FOR FREEZING
210 Calories per serving

COOK'S TIP
Polenta is a coarse-grained, yellow cornmeal which is cooked in water to form a thick paste. The quick-cook variety is suitable for this recipe. Look for it in supermarkets and also in Italian delicatessens.

COURGETTE AND PESTO 'PIZZAS'

Preparation time: 20 minutes
Cooking time: 15 minutes

SERVES 6

225 g (8 oz) courgettes
olive oil for brushing
2 beefsteak tomatoes, about 450 g (1 lb) total weight
30 ml (2 tbsp) red pesto sauce or tapénade (olive paste)
large handful of fresh basil leaves
salt and pepper
50 g (2 oz) fresh Parmesan cheese
garlic bread, to serve

1 Cut the courgettes diagonally into slices about 5 mm (¼ inch) thick. Lightly brush a non-stick frying pan with oil. Cook the courgette slices on both sides for about 5 minutes or until tender.
2 Cut each tomato into 3 slices about 1 cm (½ inch) thick and place on a lightly oiled baking sheet. Spread 5 ml (1 tsp) of pesto or tapénade on top of each slice. Place 5 or 6 basil leaves in a circle on top of the pesto.
3 Place an overlapping circle of courgettes on top of the basil leaves. Season with salt and pepper.
4 Cook at 200°C (400°F) mark 6 for 10 minutes. Top with thinly pared Parmesan cheese (see Cook's Tips). Serve immediately, accompanied with garlic bread.

NOT SUITABLE FOR FREEZING
90 Calories per serving

COOK'S TIPS
To pare fresh Parmesan cheese, use a swivel vegetable peeler.
Top each pizza with a thin slice of mozzarella at the end of step 3 – you'll need about 75 g (3 oz). Cook as directed, then brown under a hot grill.

SALAD BASKETS

Preparation time: 15 minutes
Cooking time: 12 minutes

SERVES 6

6 slices white sliced bread

50 ml (2 fl oz) olive oil

6 sun-dried tomatoes in oil plus 25 ml (1 fl oz) of the oil

2 pickled dill cucumbers, finely diced, plus 50 ml (2 fl oz) of the pickling vinegar

9 anchovy fillets, halved

75 g (3 oz) mozzarella or Edam cheese, diced

handful of small green salad leaves, preferably lamb's lettuce

flat-leaf parsley, to garnish

1 Remove the bread crusts and roll out the bread thinly with a rolling pin. Stamp or cut out a 9 cm (3½ inch) round from each slice. Brush one side lightly with a little of the olive oil. Press into deep bun tins, oiled side up, and bake at 200°C (400°F) mark 6 for 10–12 minutes. Leave to cool.

2 Finely chop 2 sun-dried tomatoes and blend with the oil and pickling vinegar.

3 Chop the remaining sun-dried tomatoes. Fill each basket with a mixture of salad leaves, tomatoes, cucumbers, anchovies and cheese. Spoon a little dressing over each basket, garnish and serve.

NOT SUITABLE FOR FREEZING
225 Calories per serving

COOK'S TIP
The baskets can be made 2–3 days ahead and stored in an airtight container. If you have no deep bun tins, use oiled ramekins.

ABOVE: SALAD BASKETS
RIGHT: ONION NOODLE SOUP (PAGE 12)

GOAT'S CHEESE PUFFS

Preparation time: 25 minutes
Cooking time: 15–20 minutes

SERVES 8

15 g (½ oz) low-fat spread, plus extra for greasing
15 ml (1 tbsp) toasted hazelnuts, finely chopped
15 ml (1 tbsp) fresh white breadcrumbs
15 ml (1 tbsp) freshly grated Parmesan cheese
15 ml (1 tbsp) plain flour
75 ml (5 tbsp) semi-skimmed milk
1 egg yolk
125 g (4 oz) soft goat's cheese, crumbled
salt and pepper
4 egg whites
2.5 ml (½ tsp) lemon juice
oil for greasing
salad leaves and nut-oil vinaigrette, to serve

1 Grease eight 150 ml (¼ pint) ramekin dishes with low-fat spread and line the bases with baking parchment.
2 Mix the nuts with the breadcrumbs and Parmesan. Use to coat the insides of the ramekins, reserving some to sprinkle on the top.
3 Melt the low-fat spread in a small saucepan. Add the flour and cook for 1 minute, stirring constantly. Remove from the heat and stir in the milk. Cook, stirring, over a moderate heat until the mixture forms a thick sauce.
4 Cool slightly, then beat in the egg yolk and goat's cheese. Season.
5 Whisk the egg whites with a pinch of salt and the lemon juice until they form stiff peaks. Fold the cheese mixture into the egg whites.
6 Divide the mixture among the dishes and top with the remaining crumb mixture. Place in a roasting tin, half fill the tin with boiling water and bake at 190°C (375°F) mark 5 for 12–15 minutes.
7 Cool for 10 minutes, then turn out, remove the paper and invert on to an oiled baking sheet.

Return to the oven or place under a hot grill to brown. Serve with salad leaves, dressed with nut-oil vinaigrette.

NOT SUITABLE FOR FREEZING
90 Calories per serving

COOK'S TIP
To prepare ahead, turn out cooked puffs, as directed. Cool, cover loosely and leave in a cool place for up to 4 hours. Reheat at 180°C (350°F) mark 4 for 15–20 minutes, then brown under a hot grill.

ONION NOODLE SOUP

Preparation time: 10 minutes
Cooking time: 40 minutes

SERVES 4

30 ml (2 tbsp) olive oil
550 g (1¼ lb) onions, skinned, quartered and sliced
1 garlic clove, skinned and crushed
125 g (4 oz) thin pasta noodles
1.1 litres (2 pints) vegetable stock
5 ml (1 tsp) plain flour
1 bunch of watercress, roughly chopped
grated rind of 1 lemon
15 ml (1 tbsp) lemon juice
salt and pepper
50 g (2 oz) Emmental cheese, grated

1 Heat the olive oil in a large, non-stick saucepan, add the onions and garlic and cook, covered, over a very low heat for 20–30 minutes or until the onions are softened and well browned.
2 Meanwhile, cook the noodles according to the packet instructions in the vegetable stock, then drain, reserving the stock.
3 Uncover the onions, increase the heat, add the

12

flour and cook, stirring, for 1 minute. Stir in the reserved vegetable stock. Bring to the boil then simmer for 5–7 minutes.

4 Stir the watercress into the soup with the lemon rind and juice and plenty of seasoning.

5 Divide the noodles among four hot bowls and spoon the soup over them. Sprinkle with Emmental cheese and serve piping hot.

NOT SUITABLE FOR FREEZING
285 Calories per serving

COOK'S TIP
Make sure the onions are well browned at the end of step 1, as this gives the soup its wonderful, rich brown colour and strong flavour.

SPICY BEAN AND COURGETTE SOUP

Preparation time: 10 minutes
Cooking time: 30 minutes

SERVES 4

30 ml (2 tbsp) olive oil
175 g (6 oz) onions, skinned and finely chopped
2 garlic cloves, skinned and crushed
10 ml (2 tsp) ground coriander
15 ml (1 tbsp) mild curry powder
450 g (1 lb) courgettes, halved and sliced
225 g (8 oz) potatoes, peeled and diced
400 g (14 oz) can red kidney beans, drained
425 g (15 oz) can flageolet beans, drained
1.4 litres (2½ pints) vegetable stock
salt and pepper
crusty bread, to serve

1 Heat the oil in a saucepan and sauté the onion and garlic for 2 minutes. Add the spices and cook, stirring, for 1 minute. Add the courgettes and potatoes and cook, stirring, for 1–2 minutes.
2 Add the remaining ingredients, cover and

simmer for 25 minutes, stirring occasionally, or until the potatoes are tender. Adjust the seasoning and serve with crusty bread.

NOT SUITABLE FOR FREEZING
290 Calories per serving

LENTIL SOUP

Preparation time: 10 minutes
Cooking time: 45 minutes

SERVES 2

50 g (2 oz) lean smoked back bacon
10 ml (2 tsp) vegetable oil
1 garlic clove, skinned and crushed
125 g (4 oz) potato, peeled and chopped
125 g (4 oz) onion, skinned and chopped
50 g (2 oz) carrot, peeled and chopped
2 celery sticks, chopped
50 g (2 oz) red lentils
300 ml (½ pint) semi-skimmed milk
300 ml (½ pint) chicken stock
salt and pepper
1 tomato, chopped

1 Trim the rind and fat from the bacon and chop into small pieces.
2 Heat the oil in a saucepan, add the bacon, garlic and vegetables and sauté for 5–10 minutes.
3 Rinse the lentils in cold water, add to the pan and cook for a further 5 minutes. Add the milk, stock and seasoning and bring to the boil. Simmer for 30 minutes, stirring occasionally.
4 Stir in the chopped tomato and cook for a further 5 minutes. Serve piping hot.

NOT SUITABLE FOR FREEZING
270 Calories per serving

CHINESE-STYLE HOT AND SOUR SOUP

Preparation time: 10 minutes
Cooking time: 20 minutes

SERVES 4

225 g (8 oz) button mushrooms, wiped and sliced
125 ml (4 fl oz) medium-dry sherry
75 ml (5 tbsp) soy sauce
30 ml (2 tbsp) chopped fresh coriander
225 g (8 oz) cooked chicken, shredded
125 g (4 oz) spring onions, trimmed and shredded
125 g (4 oz) baby sweetcorn, trimmed and halved
75 ml (5 tbsp) white wine vinegar
black pepper
coriander leaves, to garnish

1 Put the mushrooms in a large saucepan with the sherry, soy sauce, coriander and 1.1 litres (2 pints) water. Bring to the boil. Simmer, uncovered, for about 15 minutes.
2 Stir the chicken, spring onions, baby sweetcorn and wine vinegar into the saucepan. Season to taste with pepper. Simmer for a further 5 minutes. Serve hot, garnished with fresh coriander leaves.

NOT SUITABLE FOR FREEZING
150 Calories per serving

WATERCRESS SOUP

Preparation time: 15 minutes
Cooking time: 1 hour 10 minutes

SERVES 6

175 g (6 oz) leeks, trimmed and chopped
50 g (2 oz) onion, skinned and chopped
50 g (2 oz) celery, chopped
450 g (1 lb) chicken wings
50 g (2 oz) porridge oats
150 g (5 oz) watercress
30 ml (2 tbsp) skimmed milk powder (optional)
15 ml (1 tbsp) lemon juice
salt and pepper
watercress sprigs, to garnish

1 Put the leeks, onion, celery and chicken wings in a large saucepan with 1.6 litres (2¾ pints) water. Bring to the boil, cover and simmer for 1 hour.
2 Remove the chicken wings and discard. Stir in the porridge oats, then cover and simmer for a further 5 minutes. Leave to cool slightly.
3 Put the soup, watercress and skimmed milk powder, if using, in a food processor or blender and purée until smooth.
4 Return the soup to the saucepan, add the lemon juice and adjust the seasoning. Reheat, uncovered, for 1–2 minutes. Garnish with watercress sprigs and serve immediately.

NOT SUITABLE FOR FREEZING
80 Calories per serving (with skimmed milk powder)

COOK'S TIP
You can omit the skimmed milk powder if you like, but it does make the soup creamier.

WATERCRESS SOUP

TOMATO, PEPPER AND ORANGE SOUP

Preparation time: 5 minutes
Cooking time: 10 minutes

SERVES 6

400 g (14 oz) can pimientos (red peppers), drained
leaves from a few sprigs of fresh rosemary or 5 ml (1 tsp) dried rosemary
10 ml (2 tsp) caster sugar
1 litre (1¾ pints) tomato juice
300 ml (½ pint) chicken stock
450 ml (¾ pint) freshly squeezed orange juice
salt and pepper
orange slices and rosemary sprigs, to garnish

1 Purée the pimientos, rosemary, sugar and half the tomato juice in a food processor or blender.
2 Pass through a sieve into a saucepan and stir in the stock, orange juice, remaining tomato juice and seasoning.
3 Bring to the boil and simmer gently for about 10 minutes. Adjust the seasoning, garnish with orange slices and rosemary sprigs and serve.

SUITABLE FOR FREEZING AFTER STEP 2
70 Calories per serving

TOMATO AND CARDAMOM SOUP

Preparation time: 15 minutes
Cooking time: 50 minutes

SERVES 4

If available, use large beef tomatoes – they give a really good flavour.

30 ml (2 tbsp) olive oil
175 g (6 oz) onions, skinned and chopped
2 garlic cloves, skinned and crushed
275 g (10 oz) potatoes, peeled and chopped
6 green cardamom pods, split
salt and pepper
15 ml (1 tbsp) lemon juice
900 g (2 lb) fresh ripe tomatoes, chopped
100 ml (4 fl oz) dry white wine
400 g (14 oz) can chopped tomatoes
450 ml (¾ pint) chicken stock
small bunch of fresh chives, chopped
chopped fresh parsley, to garnish
raisin bread, to serve (optional)

1 Heat the oil in a large saucepan and sauté the onions for 2–3 minutes. Add the garlic, potatoes, cardamoms, seasoning and lemon juice. Cook, stirring, for 1–2 minutes.
2 Add all the remaining ingredients, except for the chives and parsley. Bring to the boil, cover and simmer for 40 minutes or until the potatoes are very tender. Cool the mixture slightly.
3 Put the soup in a food processor or blender with half the chives and purée until smooth. Rinse out the saucepan and pass the mixture through a sieve, back into the pan. Reheat gently, whisking the soup until smooth. Garnish with the remaining chives and the parsley. Serve with slices of fresh raisin bread if liked.

SUITABLE FOR FREEZING
120 Calories per serving

GREEN PEA SOUP

Preparation time: 10 minutes
Cooking time: 30 minutes

SERVES 4

25 g (1 oz) butter
225 g (8 oz) potatoes, peeled and diced
150 g (5 oz) leeks, trimmed and sliced
1 eating apple, peeled and cored
900 ml (1½ pints) chicken stock
225 g (8 oz) frozen peas
salt and pepper
60 ml (4 tbsp) crème fraîche
chopped fresh chives, to garnish
focaccia bread, to serve

1 Melt the butter in a large, heavy-based saucepan. Add the potatoes, leeks and apple and cook for about 5 minutes or until just tender.
2 Add the chicken stock and peas and bring to the boil. Reduce the heat and simmer for about 20 minutes or until the vegetables are well cooked.
3 Purée in a food processor or blender until smooth. Season to taste.
4 Add a little crème fraîche to each bowl before serving. Garnish with chopped chives and serve with warm focaccia.

SUITABLE FOR FREEZING AFTER STEP 4
150 Calories per serving

ROASTED VEGETABLE SOUP

Preparation time: 15 minutes plus chilling
Cooking time: 1–1½ hours

SERVES 8

1.4 kg (3 lb) ripe tomatoes, halved
350 g (12 oz) shallots or onions, skinned and halved
275 g (10 oz) celery, chopped
4 small garlic cloves, skinned
275 g (10 oz) carrots, peeled and sliced
4 red peppers, deseeded and cut into chunks
2 hot red chillies
60 ml (4 tbsp) olive oil
750 ml (1¼ pints) passata (see page 70)
7.5 ml (1½ tsp) sugar
grated rind of 1 lime
30 ml (2 tbsp) lime juice
salt and pepper
crushed ice and Olive and Basil Cream (see below), to serve

1 Divide all the vegetables between two roasting tins. Add the oil and stir well. Roast at 200°C (400°F) mark 6 for 1–1½ hours or until the skins are charred, turning halfway through cooking.
2 Discard the chillies. Purée the vegetables and passata in a food processor or blender, then pass through a sieve.
3 Add the sugar, lime rind and juice and plenty of seasoning. Cover and refrigerate.
4 Serve sprinkled with crushed ice and topped with Olive and Basil Cream.

SUITABLE FOR FREEZING AFTER STEP 3
165 Calories per serving

OLIVE AND BASIL CREAM

50 g (2 oz) stoned black olives
150 ml (¼ pint) crème fraîche
30 ml (2 tbsp) chopped fresh basil
grated rind of 1 lemon
10 ml (2 tsp) lemon juice
salt and pepper

1 Roughly chop the olives. Stir into the crème fraîche with the basil and lemon rind and juice. Season well. Cover and chill until ready to serve, then spoon onto the soup.

NOT SUITABLE FOR FREEZING
75 Calories per serving

GAZPACHO

Preparation time: 20 minutes plus chilling
Cooking time: nil

SERVES 6

Served chilled in summer, this is a wonderfully refreshing soup. The tomatoes must be very ripe and bright red – canned chopped tomatoes are a good substitute. Use two 400 g (14 oz) cans in the soup, but always chop some fresh tomatoes for the garnish.

1.1 kg (2½ lb) ripe red tomatoes
225 g (8 oz) onions, skinned
2 green peppers
1 large cucumber
45 ml (3 tbsp) red wine vinegar
30 ml (2 tbsp) olive oil
2.5 ml (½ tsp) sugar

2–3 garlic cloves, skinned and crushed
two 180 ml (6 fl oz) bottles tomato juice cocktail
30 ml (2 tbsp) tomato purée
salt and pepper
crushed ice, to serve

1 Roughly chop 900 g (2 lb) of the tomatoes and 125 g (4 oz) of the onions. Deseed one pepper and roughly chop. Peel three-quarters of the cucumber and roughly chop.
2 Put the prepared ingredients in a food processor or blender with the vinegar, oil, sugar, garlic, tomato juice, tomato purée and seasoning. Blend until almost smooth, then pass through a nylon sieve, pushing through as much as possible. Adjust the seasoning, cover and refrigerate.
3 Dice the remaining onion, green pepper and cucumber. Place in separate bowls, cover and chill. Peel, deseed and dice the remaining tomatoes. Place in a small bowl, cover and chill.
4 Serve the soup, well chilled, accompanied by the bowls of diced vegetables and crushed ice.

SUITABLE FOR FREEZING AFTER STEP 2
100 Calories per serving

GAZPACHO

SPINACH PARCELS ON A TOMATO COULIS

Preparation time: 15 minutes
Cooking time: 30 minutes

SERVES 6

These parcels can be served warm or cold. If spinach is not available, use a round lettuce instead.

350 g (12 oz) celeriac, peeled and diced
75 g (3 oz) Cheddar cheese, grated
25 g (1 oz) creamy fresh goat's cheese or full-fat soft cheese
salt and pepper
fresh chives, to garnish
FOR THE TOMATO COULIS
15 ml (1 tbsp) olive oil
450 g (1 lb) ripe tomatoes, chopped
15 ml (1 tbsp) tomato purée
pinch of cayenne pepper
1 bay leaf
15 ml (1 tbsp) chopped fresh basil
5 ml (1 tsp) sugar
15–30 ml (1–2 tbsp) red wine
150 ml (¼ pint) vegetable stock
16 medium-sized, fresh spinach leaves

1 Cook the celeriac in boiling salted water for 12–15 minutes or until tender. Drain, mash and beat in the grated Cheddar cheese, goat's cheese and seasoning. Leave to cool.
2 Meanwhile, make the tomato coulis. Heat the olive oil in a medium saucepan, add the tomatoes, cover and cook until soft. Add the tomato purée, cayenne pepper, bay leaf, basil, sugar, red wine and stock. Bring to the boil and simmer for 10–15 minutes. Remove the bay leaf and purée in a food processor or blender until smooth. Pass through a sieve, then season to taste. Pour into a clean pan.
3 Wash the spinach leaves and steam for 4–6 minutes or until tender. Drain on a cooling rack.
4 Slightly overlap two spinach leaves, place one-sixth of the celeriac mixture on top and wrap the leaves around to enclose it. Make six parcels. As there is a lot of filling in each parcel, you may need the extra spinach leaves in case some split.
5 Steam gently for 10 minutes or until heated through. Reheat the coulis and pour a little on to each plate. Place a spinach parcel on top, garnish with chives and serve.

NOT SUITABLE FOR FREEZING
110 Calories per serving

PRAWN AND TARRAGON OMELETTE

Preparation time: 5 minutes
Cooking time: 5 minutes

SERVES 2

4 eggs
salt and pepper
15 g (½ oz) butter
125 g (4 oz) cooked, peeled prawns
15–30 ml (1–2 tbsp) chopped fresh tarragon or 2.5 ml (½ tsp) dried tarragon

1 Whisk together the eggs, seasoning and 30 ml (2 tbsp) water.
2 Heat the butter in a medium-size non-stick omelette pan.
3 When the butter is foaming, pour in the eggs. Cook over a moderate to high heat, drawing a wooden fork through the mixture as it sets, to allow the raw egg to run through on to the pan.
4 When lightly set, sprinkle over the prawns and tarragon. Cook for a few seconds more, then fold the omelette into three. Serve immediately.

NOT SUITABLE FOR FREEZING
320 Calories per serving

COURGETTE, CHEESE AND CHIVE BAKE

Preparation time: 10 minutes
Cooking time: about 1 hour

SERVES 4

75 g (3 oz) long-grain rice
350 g (12 oz) courgettes, coarsely grated
200 ml (7 fl oz) vegetable stock
75 g (3 oz) Emmental or Leerdammer cheese, grated
3 egg whites
10 ml (2 tsp) cornflour
150 ml (¼ pint) skimmed milk
1 egg
50 g (2 oz) wafer-thin ham, chopped
15 ml (1 tbsp) chopped fresh chives
salt and pepper
salad leaves and chives, to garnish

1 Cook the rice in boiling, salted water until just tender. Drain and leave to cool. Meanwhile, simmer the courgettes in the stock for 7–10 minutes. Bring to the boil and continue to boil, uncovered, until most of the liquid has evaporated, stirring occasionally. Set aside.

2 Mix together the rice, 50 g (2 oz) of the cheese and 1 egg white. Press this mixture over the base and up the sides of a 20.5 cm (8 inch) non-stick flan tin. Cook at 180°C (350°F) mark 4 for 5–7 minutes. Leave to cool.

3 Blend together the cornflour, milk, egg and remaining 2 egg whites. Stir in the remaining cheese, ham, courgettes and chives. Season.

4 Pour the courgette mixture into the rice case and cook at 180°C (350°F) mark 4 for 35–40 minutes or until just set. Serve warm, garnished with salad leaves and chives.

NOT SUITABLE FOR FREEZING
225 Calories per serving

VEGETABLE EGG NESTS

Preparation time: 15 minutes
Cooking time: 15 minutes

SERVES 4

450 g (1 lb) leeks, trimmed and sliced
550 g (1¼ lb) courgettes, sliced
225 g (8 oz) asparagus tips
125 g (4 oz) peas
50 g (2 oz) low-fat spread
30 ml (2 tbsp) chopped fresh parsley
1 garlic clove, skinned and crushed
salt and pepper
4 eggs
8 anchovy fillets

1 Steam the leeks, courgettes and asparagus for 12–15 minutes or until tender, adding the peas for the last 5 minutes of cooking time.

2 Meanwhile, mix together the low-fat spread, parsley and garlic. Season well and set aside.

3 Poach the eggs in a saucepan of gently simmering water for 4–5 minutes or until just set.

4 Divide the hot vegetables among four individual dishes. Make a well in the centre and place an egg in each. Season each egg with pepper and cross two anchovy fillets on top. Top the vegetables with a little of the parsley and garlic mixture and serve.

NOT SUITABLE FOR FREEZING
240 Calories per serving

RICOTTA AND SPINACH GNOCCHI

Preparation time: 15 minutes
Cooking time: 10 minutes

SERVES 4

15 g (½ oz) low-fat spread
65 g (2½ oz) plain flour
450 ml (¾ pint) skimmed milk
125 g (4 oz) freshly grated Parmesan cheese
400 g (14 oz) fresh spinach or 225 g (8 oz) frozen chopped spinach, thawed
150 g (5 oz) ricotta cheese
1 egg yolk
salt and pepper
freshly grated nutmeg

1 Melt the low-fat spread in a saucepan, stir in 15 g (½ oz) of the flour and cook over a gentle heat, stirring, for 1 minute. Remove from the heat and gradually stir in the milk. Bring to the boil, stirring, until the sauce thickens. Simmer for 1–2 minutes. Stir in 25 g (1 oz) of the Parmesan cheese and keep warm.

2 Wash the spinach, put in a saucepan with only the water that clings to the leaves and cook gently for 1 minute. Drain. Chop the spinach and beat into the ricotta cheese with the remaining flour, the egg yolk and 50 g (2 oz) of the Parmesan cheese. Season to taste, adding a little nutmeg.

3 Dust the hands with flour and shape heaped teaspoons of the mixture into rounds, then drop into a saucepan of simmering salted water. The gnocchi are cooked when they float on the surface – after about 3–4 minutes. Lift out with a slotted spoon, drain and place in a lightly greased flameproof dish.

4 Spoon the sauce over the top of the gnocchi and sprinkle with the remaining Parmesan cheese. Grill until golden. Serve hot.

NOT SUITABLE FOR FREEZING
300 Calories per serving

BREAKFAST KEDGEREE

Preparation time: 10 minutes
Cooking time: 40 minutes

SERVES 4

175 g (6 oz) long-grain and wild rice, mixed
225 g (8 oz) smoked haddock fillet
150 ml (¼ pint) skimmed milk
25 g (1 oz) butter
grated rind and strained juice of 1 lemon
90 ml (6 tbsp) chopped fresh parsley
2 hard-boiled eggs, roughly chopped
salt and pepper

1 Boil the rice until tender, according to the packet instructions. Drain well.

2 Place the fish in a saucepan with the milk and 150 ml (¼ pint) water. Bring to the boil, cover and simmer for about 5 minutes or until tender. Flake the fish, discarding any skin and bones.

3 Melt the butter in a large frying pan. Add the rice, fish and lemon rind and juice. Cook over a high heat, stirring occasionally, for about 5 minutes or until piping hot.

4 Stir in the parsley and eggs and heat gently for 1 minute, to warm through. Adjust the seasoning and serve.

NOT SUITABLE FOR FREEZING
320 Calories per serving

FISH AND SHELLFISH

HOT, SWEET AND SOUR FISH AND FLAGEOLET SALAD

Preparation time: 15 minute plus cooling
Cooking time: 6–8 minutes

SERVES 4

350 g (12 oz) trout fillets
juice of 1 large orange
30 ml (2 tbsp) red wine vinegar
30 ml (2 tbsp) soy sauce
30 ml (2 tbsp) tomato purée
15 ml (1 tbsp) runny honey
5 ml (1 tsp) hot chilli powder
2.5 cm (1 inch) piece of fresh root ginger, peeled and grated
1 garlic clove, skinned and crushed
salt and pepper
400 g (14 oz) can flageolet beans, drained and rinsed
½ iceberg lettuce
handful of coriander leaves

1 Put the fish fillets in a large shallow pan and add the juice of half the orange and 150 ml (¼ pint) water. Bring the water to a simmer, cover and cook the fish gently for 6–8 minutes, until just cooked.

2 Using a fish slice, lift the fish out of the pan and leave until cool enough to handle. Remove the skin, then flake the fish into large chunks.

3 Mix the remaining orange juice with the vinegar, soy sauce, tomato purée, honey, chilli powder, ginger and garlic. Season with salt and pepper.

4 Mix the beans and fish with the dressing while the fish is still warm. Leave to cool.

5 Shred the lettuce into bite-sized pieces and mix with the beans and fish. Serve sprinkled with coriander leaves.

NOT SUITABLE FOR FREEZING
244 Calories per serving

COOK'S TIP
Omit the flageolet beans, if preferred, and serve the fish and dressing on lettuce leaves.

QUICK FISH BAKE

Preparation time: 15 minutes
Cooking time: 40 minutes

SERVES 4

This dish is based on the Greek-island dish Spetse Baked Fish, which is served in steaming casseroles. The original recipe has fresh tomatoes, herbs and sometimes wine as well. This is a simple version everyone will enjoy.

45 ml (3 tbsp) vegetable oil
350 g (12 oz) onion, skinned and chopped
1 large green pepper, deseeded and chopped
1 garlic clove, skinned and crushed
15 ml (1 tbsp) plain flour
400 g (14 oz) can chopped tomatoes with herbs
15 ml (1 tbsp) tomato purée
2.5 ml (½ tsp) dried marjoram
salt and pepper
about 550 g (1¼ lb) thick-cut cod fillet, skinned
pasta tossed in pesto, or crusty bread, to serve

1 Heat the oil in a flameproof casserole. Add the onion and sauté for 5–7 minutes until it starts to brown. Add the green pepper and garlic and sauté for a further 2–3 minutes.
2 Add the flour and cook, stirring, for 1 minute. Stir in the tomatoes, tomato purée, marjoram and plenty of seasoning. Bring to the boil, stirring.
3 Cut the fish into six or eight even-size pieces and add to the casserole. Baste with the sauce mixture.
4 Cover tightly and bake at 180°C (350°F) mark 4 for about 30 minutes or until the fish is just beginning to flake apart. Serve with pasta tossed in pesto, or with crusty bread.

NOT SUITABLE FOR FREEZING
235 Calories per serving

ROLLED PLAICE WITH PESTO

Preparation time: 30 minutes
Cooking time: 10 minutes

SERVES 4

8 small plaice fillets, about 550 g (1¼ lb) total weight
15 ml (1 tbsp) pesto sauce
30 ml (2 tbsp) lemon juice
100 ml (4 fl oz) light stock
salt and pepper
3 spring onions, trimmed and cut into 5 cm (2 inch) lengths
125 g (4 oz) fine asparagus or fine French beans, trimmed and cut into 5 cm (2 inch) lengths
125 g (4 oz) mangetouts, topped and tailed
125 g (4 oz) carrots, peeled and cut into 5 cm (2 inch) lengths
75 g (3 oz) oyster mushrooms, wiped
125 g (4 oz) baby sweetcorn, halved lengthways
30 ml (2 tbsp) vegetable oil (optional)

1 Skin the plaice fillets and divide each one along the natural centre line into two fillets. Roll up loosely (keeping the skin side on the inside).
2 Combine the pesto sauce, lemon juice, stock and seasoning. Put the plaice rolls in a saucepan and pour in the pesto mixture. Bring to the boil, cover tightly with damp baking parchment and the lid and simmer gently for about 10 minutes or until the fish is cooked.
3 Meanwhile, steam the prepared vegetables until just tender or heat the oil in a sauté pan and stir-fry for 3–4 minutes.
4 To serve, spoon the vegetables onto individual serving plates and top with the fish rolls and pan juices.

NOT SUITABLE FOR FREEZING
225 Calories per serving

TROUT MASALA

Preparation time: 15 minutes plus marinating
Cooking time: 26 minutes

SERVES 2

1 onion, skinned and chopped
2 garlic cloves, skinned
1 hot green chilli, deseeded
2.5 cm (1 inch) piece of fresh root ginger, peeled
15 ml (1 tbsp) coriander seeds
5 ml (1 tsp) ground turmeric
5 ml (1 tsp) fenugreek seeds
45 ml (3 tbsp) chopped fresh coriander
juice of 2 limes
30 ml (2 tbsp) sunflower oil
4 large tomatoes, finely chopped
15 ml (1 tbsp) garam masala
salt
2 whole trout, about 250–275 g (9–10 oz) each, cleaned, or 4 trout fillets
lime wedges, to garnish

1 Put the onion, garlic, chilli, ginger, coriander seeds, turmeric, fenugreek seeds, chopped coriander and lime juice in a blender or food processor and blend to a paste.
2 Heat the oil in a frying pan, add the spice paste and cook, stirring, for 1 minute.
3 Add the tomatoes, garam masala and salt to taste and cook for 5 minutes, until the mixture has reduced and thickened slightly. Leave to cool.
4 Using a sharp knife, make deep cuts on either side of the fish, in a criss-cross pattern. Lay the fish in a non-metallic dish, then spread the spice mixture over each side, rubbing it well into the cuts. Cover and refrigerate for 1 hour.
5 Remove the fish from the dish and place in a grill pan. Grill for about 10 minutes on each side or until firm. Garnish with lime wedges and serve.

NOT SUITABLE FOR FREEZING
335 Calories per serving

GOLDEN GRILLED SALMON

Preparation time: 10 minutes plus marinating
Cooking time: 10 minutes

SERVES 4

450 g (1 lb) salmon fillet, skinned
45 ml (3 tbsp) wholegrain mustard
30 ml (2 tbsp) olive oil
5 ml (1 tsp) white wine vinegar
grated rind and juice of 1 lemon
salt and pepper
150 ml (¼ pint) skimmed milk
2 egg yolks
new potatoes and green beans, to serve

1 Cut the salmon into 2.5 cm (1 inch) strips and put into a non-metallic dish. Mix together the mustard, oil, vinegar, lemon rind and juice and seasoning. Pour over the fish, cover and refrigerate for at least 3 hours.
2 Drain the salmon from the marinade and reserve the marinade. Grill the salmon for 3–4 minutes on each side until tender and golden brown.
3 Meanwhile, whisk the milk and egg yolks into the reserved marinade. Put into a saucepan and heat gently until the sauce thickens (do not boil). Serve at once with the grilled salmon and vegetables.

NOT SUITABLE FOR FREEZING
315 Calories per serving

CEVICHE

Preparation time: 20 minutes plus chilling
Cooking time: nil

SERVES 6

Don't be put off by the thought of raw fish – the lime juice 'cooks' the haddock. Ceviche can be made using any firm white fish, scallops or prawns, but they must be very fresh.

700 g (1½ lb) fresh haddock fillets
15 ml (1 tbsp) coriander seeds
5 ml (1 tsp) black peppercorns
juice of 6 limes
5 ml (1 tsp) salt
1 hot red chilli, deseeded and chopped
225 g (8 oz) cucumber, thinly sliced
2 small avocados, peeled and thickly sliced
1 bunch of spring onions, trimmed and shredded
few drops of Tabasco sauce
45 ml (3 tbsp) chopped fresh coriander
salt and pepper

1 Cut the haddock diagonally into 1 cm (½ inch) thick strips and place in a non-metallic bowl.
2 Crush the coriander seeds and black peppercorns to a fine powder in a pestle and mortar, or put in a strong bowl and crush with the end of a rolling pin. Sieve to remove the seed husks, then mix with the lime juice, salt and chilli. Pour over the haddock. Cover and refrigerate for at least 24 hours (the longer the better), stirring lightly from time to time.
3 To serve, drain the fish from the marinade, discarding the liquid. Mix the cucumber, avocados and spring onions with the fish. Add the Tabasco sauce and fresh coriander and season to taste. Serve chilled.

NOT SUITABLE FOR FREEZING
140 Calories per serving

COCONUT FISH PILAU

Preparation time: 10 minutes
Cooking time: 30 minutes

SERVES 4

175 g (6 oz) cod fillet, skinned
15 ml (1 tbsp) olive oil
125 g (4 oz) onion, skinned and chopped
1 garlic clove, skinned and crushed
15 ml (1 tbsp) Thai green curry paste, or Indian curry paste
225 g (8 oz) Thai fragrant rice or basmati rice
600 ml (1 pint) fish stock
150 ml (¼ pint) coconut milk
125 g (4 oz) sugar-snap peas, blanched
125 g (4 oz) cooked, peeled tiger prawns
25 g (1 oz) toasted blanched almonds
15 ml (1 tbsp) lemon juice
salt and pepper
chopped fresh coriander, to garnish

1 Cut the cod fillet into large, bite-size pieces.
2 Heat the oil in a large, non-stick frying pan. Add the onion and garlic and cook for 4–5 minutes until golden. Stir in the curry paste and cook, stirring, for 1–2 minutes.
3 Add the rice, stock and coconut milk. Bring to the boil. Cover and simmer gently for about 15 minutes, stirring occasionally with a fork.
4 When the rice is tender and most of the liquid has been absorbed, add the cod. Cook for a further 3–5 minutes or until the fish is cooked through.
5 Stir in the sugar-snap peas, prawns, almonds, lemon juice and seasoning. Heat gently for about 1 minute, to warm through, then serve immediately, garnished with coriander.

NOT SUITABLE FOR FREEZING
375 Calories per serving

CEVICHE

COD IN ORANGE AND CIDER SAUCE

Preparation time: 10 minutes
Cooking time: 30 minutes

SERVES 4

4 cod fillets, about 175 g (6 oz) each, skinned
175 g (6 oz) onion, skinned and chopped
pared rind of 1 orange
black pepper
30 ml (2 tbsp) orange juice
150 ml (¼ pint) medium-dry cider
100 ml (4 fl oz) fish stock
10 ml (2 tsp) chopped fresh coriander
coriander sprigs, to garnish

1 Place the fish in a shallow ovenproof dish. Place the onion and orange rind on top of the fish and season with black pepper.
2 Mix the orange juice with the cider and fish stock. Pour over the fish, cover and bake at 190°C (375°F) mark 5 for 20–25 minutes or until the fish is cooked through.
3 Carefully place the fish, onion and orange rind in a serving dish and keep warm.
4 Strain the cooking liquid into a small saucepan and boil rapidly for about 5 minutes or until the liquid is reduced by half. Pour over the fish and sprinkle with coriander. Garnish with coriander and serve immediately.

NOT SUITABLE FOR FREEZING
160 Calories per serving

SWEET AND SOUR MONKFISH KEBABS

Preparation time:15 minutes plus marinating
Cooking time: 10–12 minutes

SERVES 4

Monkfish is ideal for kebabs as its firm flesh doesn't fall off skewers.

225 g (8 oz) streaky bacon
450 g (1 lb) monkfish fillet, skinned and cut into bite-size pieces
1 small aubergine, about 225 g (8 oz), cut into chunks
2 small red onions, skinned
2 lemons or limes, sliced
15 ml (1 tbsp) lemon juice
30 ml (2 tbsp) runny honey
15 ml (1 tbsp) soy sauce
15 ml (1 tbsp) tomato purée
salt and pepper
frisée lettuce, to garnish

1 Stretch the bacon rashers with the back of a knife and cut each one into three. Wrap a piece of bacon around each piece of fish.
2 Blanch the aubergine in boiling, salted water for 1 minute. Drain and dry on absorbent kitchen paper. Quarter the onions, then separate each quarter into two to give thinner pieces.
3 Thread the fish, onions, aubergines and lemon or lime slices on to eight skewers. Place the kebabs side by side in a non-metallic dish.
4 Whisk together the lemon juice, honey, soy sauce, tomato purée and seasoning. Spoon over the kebabs, cover and marinate in the refrigerator for at least 12 hours, turning once.
5 Place the kebabs in a grill pan. Brush with a little of the marinade and grill for 10–12 minutes, turning occasionally, until all the ingredients are tender. Garnish with frisée lettuce and serve.

NOT SUITABLE FOR FREEZING
355 Calories per serving

CREAMY FISH AND PUMPKIN PIE

Preparation time: 10 minutes
Cooking time: 30 minutes

SERVES 4

700 g (1½ lb) pumpkin or squash, peeled and chopped

350 g (12 oz) courgettes, chopped

450 g (1 lb) cod fillet, skinned and cut into large chunks

100 ml (4 fl oz) skimmed milk

3 peppercorns

1 bay leaf

40 g (1½ oz) low-fat spread

45 ml (3 tbsp) plain flour

50 ml (2 fl oz) dry white wine

75 g (3 oz) low-fat soft cheese with garlic and herbs

30 ml (2 tbsp) chopped fresh tarragon or 5 ml (1 tsp) dried tarragon

salt and pepper

4 sheets of filo pastry, about 50 g (2 oz) total weight

15 ml (1 tbsp) sesame seeds

1 Simmer the pumpkin in salted water for 5 minutes. Add the courgettes and simmer for a further 5 minutes, or until just tender. Drain well.

2 Meanwhile, put the cod in a saucepan with the milk, peppercorns, bay leaf and 200 ml (7 fl oz) water. Bring to the boil and simmer for about 2 minutes, until just tender. Drain well, reserving the cooking liquor.

3 Melt 30 g (1 oz) low-fat spread in a saucepan, add the flour and cook, stirring, for 1 minute. Gradually stir in the reserved cooking liquor and the wine. Remove from the heat and add the cheese, tarragon and seasoning.

4 Place the vegetables and fish in a 1.1 litre (2 pint) ovenproof dish. Spoon over the sauce. Crumple the filo pastry and place on top. Melt the remaining low-fat spread and brush over the pastry. Sprinkle with sesame seeds.

5 Bake at 200°C (400°F) Mark 6 for about 15 minutes until golden brown and piping hot.

NOT SUITABLE FOR FREEZING
300 Calories per serving

LIGHT SEAFOOD SAUTÉ

Preparation time: 15 minutes
Cooking time: 15 minutes

SERVES 4

30 ml (2 tbsp) olive oil

450 g (1 lb) monkfish fillet, skinned and cut into bite-size pieces

1 bunch of spring onions, trimmed and sliced

1 garlic clove, skinned and finely chopped

2.5 cm (1 inch) piece of fresh root ginger, peeled and finely chopped

275 g (10 oz) trimmed leeks, sliced

1 red pepper, deseeded and chopped

125 g (4 oz) cooked, peeled prawns

15 ml (1 tbsp) each hoisin sauce, light soy sauce and dry sherry

black pepper

1 Heat the oil in a large frying pan, add the monkfish and sauté for 2–3 minutes. Remove with a slotted spoon.

2 Add the onions, garlic and ginger and sauté for 2 minutes or until beginning to soften. Add the leeks and red pepper and sauté for 10 minutes, stirring, until softened.

3 Return the monkfish to the pan with the prawns, hoisin sauce, soy sauce and sherry. Season with plenty of black pepper (the soy sauce is quite salty). Cook, stirring, for 30 seconds–1 minute. Serve immediately.

NOT SUITABLE FOR FREEZING
230 Calories per serving

SALMON WITH SALSA FRESCA

Preparation time: 20 minutes plus marinating
Cooking time: 10 minutes

SERVES 6

**6 skinless, boneless salmon fillets, about 700 g
(1½ lb) total weight**
1 large garlic clove, skinned and crushed
grated rind of 1 lemon
15 ml (1 tbsp) lemon juice
15 ml (1 tbsp) sun-dried tomato paste
150 ml (¼ pint) low-fat natural yogurt
lime slices, to garnish

FOR THE SALSA FRESCA
**1 large hot green chilli, deseeded and finely
chopped**
175 g (6 oz) cucumber, finely chopped
grated rind and juice of 1 lime
2 spring onions, trimmed and chopped
350 g (12 oz) cherry tomatoes, chopped
5 ml (1 tsp) low-calorie sweetener
salt and pepper
small handful of chopped fresh mint leaves

1 Mix together the garlic, lemon rind and juice,
sun-dried tomato paste and yogurt.
2 Thoroughly coat the salmon on both sides with
the marinade and place in a non-metallic dish.
Cover loosely and refrigerate for at least 3 hours.
3 To make the salsa fresca, combine all the
ingredients except the mint and season well.
Cover and refrigerate for about 2 hours.
4 Place the salmon on a baking sheet and cook
under a hot grill for about 10 minutes. There is no
need to turn the fish over – allow it to turn golden
brown on top and it will cook through.
5 Stir the mint into the salsa. Garnish the salmon
with lime slices and serve with salsa fresca.

NOT SUITABLE FOR FREEZING
236 Calories per serving

GRILLED RED MULLET

Preparation time: 15 minutes plus marinating
Cooking time: 10–15 minutes

SERVES 4

4 red mullet, thawed if frozen
black pepper
12 sprigs of rosemary
juice of 1 lemon
30 ml (2 tbsp) red wine vinegar
10 ml (2 tsp) Worcestershire sauce
10 ml (2 tsp) runny honey
45 ml (3 tbsp) corn oil
10 ml (2 tsp) chopped fresh rosemary leaves
rosemary sprigs, to garnish
brown rice and peas, to serve

1 Remove the scales from the fish by scraping
from tail to head with the back of a knife. Rinse
well. Sprinkle pepper inside each fish and put
1 sprig of rosemary in each one. Arrange in a
flameproof dish.
2 Mix together the lemon juice, vinegar,
Worcestershire sauce, honey, oil and chopped
rosemary and pour over the fish. Cover and leave
to marinate for 30 minutes, turning once.
3 Remove the fish from the marinade and arrange
on a grill rack. Place more rosemary sprigs on top
and cook under a medium grill for 10–15 minutes,
turning carefully once and brushing with the
marinade.
4 Discard the rosemary sprigs and garnish with
fresh rosemary. Serve with brown rice and peas.

NOT SUITABLE FOR FREEZING
277 Calories per serving

SALMON WITH SALSA FRESCA

BAKED COD WITH HORSERADISH AND TARTARE SAUCE

Preparation time: 20 minutes
Cooking time: 15–20 minutes

SERVES 6

These cod steaks, baked with a crumbed crust flavoured with fresh horseradish, lemon and herbs, are served with a low-fat tartare sauce. If you cannot obtain fresh horseradish, then horseradish sauce can be used as an alternative (see Variation). If possible, buy fresh rather than pre-packed cod. If it's very fresh, the cooked fish will have very white flakes, and an almost milky liquid will ooze out during cooking.

50 g (2 oz) crustless wholemeal bread
grated rind of 1 lemon
30 ml (2 tbsp) chopped fresh parsley
50 g (2 oz) freshly grated horseradish
salt and pepper
6 cod steaks, about 125 g (4 oz) each
FOR THE TARTARE SAUCE
6 gherkins, finely chopped
225 g (8 oz) low-fat crème fraîche
30 ml (2 tbsp) chopped fresh parsley
30 ml (2 tbsp) chopped fresh dill
10–15 ml (2–3 tbsp) lemon juice
lemon slices and dill sprigs, to garnish

1 Place the bread in a food processor and process until medium to fine breadcrumbs are formed. (Alternatively, use a grater). Place the breadcrumbs in a large bowl.
2 Add the lemon rind, parsley, horseradish and seasoning.
3 Place the cod steaks in a shallow roasting tin and season with salt and pepper. Top the steaks with the crumb mixture and press on firmly. Bake at 200°C (400°F) mark 6 for 15–20 minutes until the steaks are tender.

4 Meanwhile, make the tartare sauce. Stir the gherkins into the crème fraîche with the parsley and dill. Add lemon juice to taste and mix well.
5 Place the cod steaks on warmed serving plates, garnish with lemon slices and dill sprigs and serve topped with a spoonful of the tartare sauce.

NOT SUITABLE FOR FREEZING
210 Calories per serving

VARIATION
If fresh horseradish is unobtainable, substitute horseradish sauce, but remember that this will increase the calorie count slightly. Spread 10 ml (2 tsp) over each cod steak then top with the breadcrumbs mixed with the lemon rind, parsley and seasoning. You can also use this crust on other mild flavoured fish, such as salmon or halibut.

SPICED FISH STIR-FRY

Preparation time: 20 minutes
Cooking time: 10 minutes

SERVES 4

If monkfish is not available, use haddock fillet instead, although it will break up more readily during cooking.

225 g (8 oz) monkfish fillet, skinned
225 g (8 oz) scallops
5 ml (1 tsp) plain flour
10 ml (2 tsp) ground coriander
10 ml (2 tsp) ground cumin
1 small green pepper, deseeded and thinly sliced
1 small yellow pepper, deseeded and thinly sliced
1 onion, skinned and thinly sliced

225 g (8 oz) tomatoes, skinned and cut into eighths
30 ml (2 tbsp) olive oil
125 g (4 oz) beansprouts
75 ml (5 tbsp) dry white wine
15 ml (1 tbsp) chopped fresh coriander
salt and pepper
rice or noodles, to serve

1 Cut the monkfish into thin strips. Remove the orange roe from the scallops and slice the scallops into thin rounds. Mix together the flour and spices and use to coat the fish, scallop slices and scallop roe.

2 Heat half the oil in a frying pan. Add the peppers and onion and stir-fry over a high heat until beginning to brown. Add the tomatoes and beansprouts and cook for 2–3 minutes, or until the tomatoes begin to soften.

3 Meanwhile, heat the remaining oil in another frying pan. Add the fish and stir-fry for 2–3 minutes.

4 Add the fish to the vegetable mixture. Add the wine, coriander and seasoning and heat until bubbling. Serve immediately with boiled rice or noodles.

NOT SUITABLE FOR FREEZING
180 Calories per serving

HOT AND SOUR FISH

Preparation time: 10 minutes
Cooking time: 8 minutes

SERVES 4

15 ml (1 tbsp) olive oil
5 ml (1 tsp) ground turmeric
50 g (2 oz) onion, skinned and finely chopped
1 hot green chilli, deseeded and finely chopped
225 g (8 oz) courgettes, thinly sliced
50 g (2 oz) frozen peas
350 g (12 oz) haddock fillet, skinned and cut into bite-size pieces
10 ml (2 tsp) lemon juice
60 ml (4 tbsp) hoisin sauce
salt and pepper
noodles, to serve

1 Heat the oil in a large frying pan. Add the turmeric, onion, chilli, courgettes and peas and stir-fry over a high heat for 4–5 minutes or until the vegetables begin to soften.

2 Add the fish to the pan with the lemon juice, hoisin sauce and 150 ml (¼ pint) water. Bring to the boil and simmer, uncovered, for 2–3 minutes or until the fish is just tender. Season. Serve immediately with freshly cooked noodles.

NOT SUITABLE FOR FREEZING
135 Calories per serving

COOK'S TIP
Hoisin sauce is ideal for brushing over fish and chicken before grilling.

MUSSELS WITH GINGER, CHILLI AND CORIANDER

Preparation time: 20 minutes
Cooking time: 10 minutes

SERVES 4

A delicious, spicy alternative to moules marinières. If you prefer a creamy sauce, opt for one of the variations. Make sure you clean the mussels thoroughly, discarding any that remain open after being given a sharp tap.

1 kg (2¼ lb) mussels

15 g (½ oz) fresh coriander

1 bunch of spring onions, trimmed and shredded

2 garlic cloves, skinned and finely chopped

25 g (1 oz) fresh root ginger, peeled and finely chopped

1 small hot red chilli, deseeded and cut into fine strips

150 ml (¼ pint) white wine

40 g (1½ oz) butter, diced

coriander sprigs, to garnish

1 Scrub the mussels thoroughly under cold running water, pulling away the beards from the sides of the shells. Discard mussels with damaged shells, or any that don't close when tapped with the back of a knife. Put the mussels in a colander and set aside.

2 Strip the leaves from the coriander and set aside; reserve the stalks. Put the spring onions, garlic, ginger, chilli and coriander stalks in a saucepan which is large enough to hold the mussels. Add the wine and 150 ml (¼ pint) water. Bring to the boil and simmer for 2 minutes.

3 Add the mussels to the pan, cover with a tight-fitting lid and cook over a moderate heat, shaking the pan occasionally, for 4–5 minutes, until the shells open. Turn the mussels into a colander set over a bowl. Discard the coriander stalks and any unopened mussels.

4 Pour the liquid from the bowl back into the pan. Place over a low heat and whisk in the butter, a piece at a time. Add the coriander leaves.

5 Transfer the mussels to warmed individual serving dishes and pour over the sauce. Serve immediately, garnished with coriander sprigs.

NOT SUITABLE FOR FREEZING
175 Calories per serving

VARIATIONS
Stir in 60–75 ml (4–5 tbsp) crème fraîche instead of the butter.
Replace the white wine with 150 ml (¼ pint) coconut milk.

MUSSELS WITH GINGER, CHILLI AND CORIANDER

GRILLED MONKFISH WITH LEMON AND DILL

Preparation time: 15 minutes plus marinating
Cooking time: 12 minutes

SERVES 4

700 g (1½ lb) monkfish tail or other firm white fish
45 ml (3 tbsp) fresh lemon juice
15 ml (1 tbsp) chopped fresh dill or 2.5 ml (½ tsp) dried dill
45 ml (3 tbsp) olive oil
2 garlic cloves, skinned and sliced
salt and pepper
lemon slices, to garnish
French beans and fennel, to serve

1 Remove all membrane from the monkfish and cut out the backbone to give two long fillets. Cut these in half to give four 'steaks'. Place in a non-metallic dish.

2 Whisk together the remaining ingredients and season well. Pour over the fish, cover and leave in a cool place for at least 4 hours, turning occasionally.

3 Remove the fish from the marinade, arrange on a wire rack in a grill pan and grill for about 6 minutes on each side, basting regularly with the marinade. Serve immediately, accompanied by French beans and fennel, and garnished with lemon slices.

NOT SUITABLE FOR FREEZING
200 Calories per serving

COOK'S TIP

If you are short of time, you can cook the fish without marinating it, but the lemon and dill will not give as much flavour to the fish.

GRILLED TURBOT WITH CHERVIL AND TOMATO SAUCE

Preparation time: 10 minutes
Cooking time: 10 minutes

SERVES 4

300 ml (½ pint) milk
1 slice of onion
1 blade of mace
4–6 black peppercorns
15 g (½ oz) butter
15 g (½ oz) plain flour
salt and pepper
5 ml (1 tsp) tomato purée
60 ml (4 tbsp) chopped fresh chervil
8 small turbot steaks
melted butter for brushing
2 tomatoes, skinned and cut into thin strips
5–10 ml (1–2 tsp) lemon juice
fresh chervil sprigs, to garnish

1 Place the milk in a small saucepan with the onion slice, mace and peppercorns. Bring to the boil and remove from the heat. Cover and leave to infuse for about 10 minutes. Strain.

2 Melt the butter in a small saucepan. Add the flour and cook, stirring, for 1 minute. Gradually stir in the strained milk and seasoning. Bring to the boil, stirring constantly. Simmer gently for a few minutes. Add the tomato purée and chervil.

3 Meanwhile, brush the turbot steaks with melted butter and grill for 5–6 minutes on each side.

4 Add the tomato strips to the sauce. Add lemon juice to taste and a little more milk, if necessary. Garnish the grilled turbot steaks with chervil sprigs and serve with the sauce.

NOT SUITABLE FOR FREEZING
280 Calories per serving

CRISPY FISH PIE

Preparation time: 30 minutes
Cooking time: 50 minutes

SERVES 6

350 g (12 oz) spinach
225 ml (8 fl oz) milk
225 g (8 oz) haddock fillet
225 g (8 oz) smoked haddock fillet
125 g (4 oz) butter
30 ml (2 tbsp) plain white flour
salt and pepper
1 hard-boiled egg, chopped
275 g (10 oz) filo pastry, each sheet about 19 x 38 cm (7½ x 15 inches)
75 g (3 oz) long-grain rice, cooked and cooled

1 Wash the spinach, discarding any coarse stalks. Place the leaves in a saucepan with only the water that clings to them. Cover tightly and cook over a moderate heat for 5–6 minutes or until the spinach is tender. Drain, squeezing out excess liquid. Roughly chop and leave to cool.
2 Put the milk in a saucepan, add the fish and poach gently for 10 minutes, until just cooked. Drain, reserving the cooking liquor. Flake the fish into large pieces, discarding any skin and bones.
3 Melt 40 g (1½ oz) butter in a saucepan, add the flour and cook, stirring, for 1–2 minutes. Gradually stir in the reserved liquor, bring to the boil and simmer for 1–2 minutes until thickened. Carefully stir in the fish and chopped egg. Season then leave to cool.
4 Melt the remaining butter. Cut each filo sheet into three equal portions, about 12.5 x 19 cm (5 x 7½ inches).
5 Brush a baking sheet with melted butter then place one pastry sheet on it. Brush lightly with butter and continue layering like this until half the pastry has been used.
6 Spoon the rice onto the pastry, leaving a 2.5 cm (1 inch) border all round. Cover the rice with spinach and then top with the fish mixture.

7 Place a sheet of the remaining pastry on top of the filling and brush with butter then complete the layering as above. Seal the edges well and brush the top with the remaining butter.
8 Bake at 200°C (400°F) mark 6 for about 30 minutes, covering with foil if necessary to prevent over-browning, until the pie is crisp and golden brown in colour and heated through.

NOT SUITABLE FOR FREEZING
335 Calories per serving

FISH STEAKS IN LIME

Preparation time: 10 minutes plus marinating
Cooking time: 16 minutes

SERVES 4

grated rind and juice of 4 limes
30 ml (2 tbsp) chopped fresh basil or 15 ml (1 tbsp) dried basil
75 ml (3 fl oz) dry white wine
2 garlic cloves, skinned and crushed
5 ml (1 tsp) paprika
15 ml (1 tbsp) sunflower oil
black pepper
4 cod steaks, about 175 g (6 oz) each
lime slices and chopped basil leaves, to garnish

1 Mix together the lime rind and juice, basil, wine, garlic, paprika and oil and season with black pepper. Put the fish steaks in a non-metallic dish and spoon over the marinade. Leave to marinate for at least 2 hours, turning at least once.
2 Remove the steaks from the marinade. Cook under the grill for 8 minutes on each side, basting with the marinade, until the fish is cooked through and the flesh flakes easily. Serve immediately, garnished with the lime slices and basil.

NOT SUITABLE FOR FREEZING
175 Calories per serving

MEDITERRANEAN FISH CASSEROLE

Preparation time: 15 minutes
Cooking time: 45 minutes

SERVES 4

This dish is so light you can have a glass of wine with it and the calories are only just over 300 per serving. A few prawns could be stirred into this casserole at the end of stage 2: 125 g (4 oz) would add an extra 134 calories per portion.

25 g (1 oz) low-fat spread
175 g (6 oz) onion, skinned and chopped
1 small green pepper, about 125 g (4 oz), deseeded and chopped
225 g (8 oz) broccoli florets
10 ml (2 tsp) paprika
15 ml (1 tbsp) plain flour
50 ml (2 fl oz) dry white wine
50 ml (2 fl oz) light stock
225 g (8 oz) tomatoes, chopped
15 ml (1 tbsp) tomato purée
5 ml (1 tsp) dried basil
1 garlic clove, skinned and crushed
salt and pepper
450 g (1 lb) haddock fillet, skinned and cut into 5 cm (2 inch) pieces
dry white wine, to accompany

1 Melt the low-fat spread in a large flameproof casserole, add the onion, pepper and broccoli and stir-fry over a high heat for 2–3 minutes.
2 Add the paprika and flour and cook, stirring, for 1 minute. Add the wine, stock, tomatoes, tomato purée, basil, garlic and seasoning and bring to the boil.
3 Add the fish, cover tightly and cook at 170°C (325°F) mark 3 for about 40 minutes or until the fish is tender. Adjust the seasoning and serve.

NOT SUITABLE FOR FREEZING
310 Calories per serving with a glass of wine

LEMON SOLE WITH MOUSSELINE SAUCE

Preparation time: 5 minutes
Cooking time: 6 minutes

SERVES 6

This rich butter sauce is the perfect partner for plain grilled sole.

2 egg yolks
10 ml (2 tsp) lemon juice
salt and pepper
50 g (2 oz) unsalted butter, softened
melted butter for brushing
12 single lemon sole fillets
50 ml (2 fl oz) whipping cream
mangetouts, to serve

1 Place the egg yolks in a small bowl. Add 5 ml (1 tsp) of the lemon juice, salt and pepper and a knob of the softened butter.
2 Place the bowl over a saucepan of simmering water. Heat gently, whisking constantly, until the mixture is quite thick.
3 Remove the bowl from the saucepan. Whisk in the rest of the softened butter, a small piece at a time. Add the remaining lemon juice. Keep the sauce warm by replacing the bowl over the saucepan and heating very gently.
4 Brush the sole fillets with melted butter and grill for 2–3 minutes per side.
5 Fold the whisked cream into the sauce. Serve immediately, spooned over the fillets, and accompanied by mangetouts.

NOT SUITABLE FOR FREEZING
260 Calories per serving

MEDITERRANEAN FISH CASSEROLE

MEAT AND POULTRY

PORK WITH CRUNCHY RED CABBAGE

Preparation time: 10 minutes plus marinating
Cooking time: 15 minutes

SERVES 4

Balsamic vinegar is expensive but a little goes a long way. It's great for adding to rich, meaty soups and casseroles – only a drop or two is needed. The combination of red cabbage, onions and apples in this dish makes it high in fibre. High-fibre foods are a good choice for slimmers as they are more satisfying and help to stave off hunger. Red cabbage, in common with all highly coloured vegetables, is an excellent source of the anti-oxidant vitamins beta carotene and vitamin C.

4 thin, lean pork chops, about 700 g (1½ lb) total weight
60 ml (4 tbsp) vinegar, preferably balsamic
45 ml (3 tbsp) chopped fresh herbs, eg parsley or sage
15 ml (1 tbsp) runny honey
30 ml (2 tbsp) lemon juice
salt and pepper

15 ml (1 tbsp) olive oil
175 g (6 oz) red onion, skinned and sliced
1 garlic clove, skinned and crushed
225 g (8 oz) red cabbage, finely shredded
2 red apples, cored and sliced

1 Trim the pork and make lattice cuts in one side. Place in a shallow, non-metallic dish. Mix together 30 ml (2 tbsp) balsamic vinegar, the chopped herbs, 10 ml (2 tsp) honey, 15 ml (1 tbsp) lemon juice and seasoning. Spoon over the pork chops. Cover and marinate for at least 30 minutes.
2 Heat the oil in a large frying pan. Sauté the onions and crushed garlic for 2 minutes. Add the cabbage, apples and the remaining vinegar, lemon juice and honey. Season well. Cook, stirring, over a moderate heat for 4–5 minutes or until the liquid has evaporated. Keep warm over a low heat.
3 Meanwhile, grill the chops for 4–5 minutes on each side or until cooked through, basting with the marinade. Serve with the red cabbage.

RED CABBAGE SUITABLE FOR FREEZING
295 Calories per serving

LEMON-ROASTED PORK WITH GARLIC AND BASIL

Preparation time: 15 minutes plus marinating
Cooking time: 35 minutes

SERVES 6

2 pork tenderloins, about 350 g (12 oz) each
grated rind and strained juice of 2 lemons
90 ml (6 tbsp) chopped fresh basil or parsley
12 garlic cloves, skinned and blanched
salt and pepper
2–3 fresh bay leaves
30 ml (2 tbsp) olive oil
fresh bay leaves, fresh herbs and lemon slices, to garnish

1 Trim the pork of excess fat. Make a deep lengthways cut in each fillet and open out flat. Sprinkle the lemon rind over the pork. Sprinkle on the basil. Cut any large garlic cloves in half. Lay them evenly down the middle of each fillet. Season.

2 Close the tenderloins and tie loosely at 2.5 cm (1 inch) intervals with string. Place in a shallow, non-metallic dish with the bay leaves and the lemon juice. Cover and marinate in the refrigerator overnight.

3 Remove the pork from the dish and reserve the marinade. Heat the oil in a sauté pan and cook the meat until browned all over. Transfer to a shallow roasting tin with the marinade. Season. Cook in the oven at 200°C (400°F) mark 6 for 35 minutes, basting frequently. Alternatively, cook over a barbecue for 30–35 minutes, turning frequently and brushing with the marinade.

4 Slice the pork, garnish with bay leaves, fresh herbs and a few lemon slices and serve.

NOT SUITABLE FOR FREEZING
170 Calories per serving

SATAY-STYLE PORK

Preparation time: 20 minutes
Cooking time: 10 minutes

SERVES 4

This simple dish is ideal for a light snack or served as part of a buffet.

450 g (1 lb) pork fillet, cubed
90 ml (6 tbsp) Greek yogurt
90 ml (6 tbsp) bottled satay marinade
15 ml (1 tbsp) lemon juice
5 ml (1 tsp) ground cumin
15 ml (1 tbsp) vegetable oil
salt and pepper
lemon slices and mint, to garnish

1 Put the pork in a bowl and add the remaining ingredients. Stir well to coat the pork in the mixture, cover and refrigerate for at least 15 minutes.

2 Thread the meat on to four skewers and brush with the marinade. Grill for about 10 minutes until cooked through, turning and basting occasionally.

3 Put the remaining marinade in a small saucepan and heat very gently, taking care not to let it boil. Pour over the meat, garnish with lemon slices and mint and serve.

NOT SUITABLE FOR FREEZING
250 Calories per serving

SWEET AND SPICY PORK

Preparation time: 5 minutes
Cooking time: 35 minutes

SERVES 6

425 g (15 oz) can pineapple pieces in natural juice
700 g (1½ lb) pork tenderloin or 4 pork steaks
15 ml (1 tbsp) olive oil
2 garlic cloves, skinned and crushed
15 ml (1 tbsp) mild curry paste
30 ml (2 tbsp) lemon juice
30 ml (2 tbsp) mango chutney
lentils with chopped parsley, to serve

1 Drain the pineapple pieces, reserving the juice. Roughly chop the pineapple.
2 Heat a non-stick frying pan and dry-fry the pork tenderloin over a high heat for 4 minutes or until golden brown. Transfer to a small ovenproof dish and set aside.

3 Lower the heat and add the oil, garlic and curry paste and cook for 30 seconds. Stir in the pineapple and juice, lemon juice and chutney. Bring to the boil, then pour immediately over the pork.
4 Cook at 200°C (400°F) mark 6 for about 25 minutes, basting occasionally. Slice thickly and serve with the pineapple and mango sauce and lentils and parsley.

COOK'S TIPS
Omit the oil if using pork steaks – they should leave enough fat in the pan for frying the garlic and curry paste.
If you'd like a slightly thicker sauce, bubble the pan juices in a saucepan until reduced by half.

NOT SUITABLE FOR FREEZING
240 Calories per serving

ABOVE: SWEET AND SPICY PORK
RIGHT: HARVEST PORK CASSEROLE (PAGE 44)

HARVEST PORK CASSEROLE

Preparation time: 15 minutes
Cooking time: 1¾ hours

SERVES 6

700 g (1½ lb) boneless leg of pork
45 ml (3 tbsp) olive oil
225 g (8 oz) onion, skinned and chopped
1 garlic clove, skinned and crushed
450 g (1 lb) parsnips, peeled, halved and sliced
15 ml (1 tbsp) ground coriander
5 ml (1 tsp) cumin seeds or 15 ml (1 tbsp) ground cumin
30 ml (2 tbsp) plain flour
300 ml (½ pint) beef stock
300 ml (½ pint) apple juice or cider
salt and pepper
2 small, crisp, red eating apples, cored and chopped
chopped fresh chives, to garnish

1 Trim the pork of excess fat and cut into bite-size pieces. Heat the oil in a flameproof casserole and cook the meat until well browned. Remove with a slotted spoon and drain on absorbent kitchen paper.

2 Add the onion and garlic and sauté for 2–3 minutes. Add the parsnips, coriander and cumin and sauté for 2 minutes. Add the flour and cook, stirring, for 1 minute. Remove from the heat and gradually add the stock, apple juice and seasoning.

3 Bring to the boil and return the meat to the casserole. Cover and cook at 170°C (325°F) mark 3 for 1¼ hours or until the pork is almost tender.

4 Add the apples, cover and cook for 15–20 minutes or until the pork is tender. Adjust the seasoning, garnish with chives and serve.

SUITABLE FOR FREEZING AT THE END OF STEP 3
335 Calories per serving

PORK AND WATERCRESS CASSEROLE

Preparation time: 5 minutes
Cooking time: 45 minutes

SERVES 4

Choose the leanest pork chops and trim off any excess fat if necessary.

30 ml (2 tbsp) olive oil
4 thin lean pork chops, about 150 g (5 oz) each
125 g (4 oz) onion, skinned and chopped
7.5 ml (1½ tsp) ground cumin
7.5 ml (1½ tsp) ground coriander
pinch of ground cardamom
15 ml (1 tbsp) plain flour
grated rind of 1 lemon
300 ml (½ pint) stock
1 bunch of watercress, finely chopped
salt and pepper
30 ml (2 tbsp) single cream
watercress sprigs, to garnish
boiled rice and carrot sticks, to serve

1 Heat the oil in a large flameproof casserole and cook the chops until browned on both sides. Drain on absorbent kitchen paper. Add the onion and sauté for 2–3 minutes. Add the spices, flour and lemon rind and then cook, stirring, for 1–2 minutes.

2 Stir in the stock, watercress and seasoning and bring to the boil.

3 Return the chops to the casserole, cover and bake at 180°C (350°F) mark 4 for about 40 minutes or until tender. Add the single cream and heat gently to warm through: do not boil. Garnish with watercress sprigs and serve with boiled rice and carrot sticks.

SUITABLE FOR FREEZING BEFORE ADDING THE CREAM
300 Calories per serving

PORK TENDERLOIN WITH ORANGE

Preparation time: 5 minutes plus marinating
Cooking time: 25 minutes

SERVES 6

grated rind of 1 orange and 1 lemon
50 ml (2 fl oz) each orange and lemon juice
2.5 cm (1 inch) piece of fresh root ginger, peeled and grated
15 ml (1 tbsp) hoisin sauce
5 ml (1 tsp) runny honey
1 garlic clove, skinned and crushed
700 g (1½ lb) pork tenderloin
5 ml (1 tsp) vegetable oil
300 ml (½ pint) chicken stock
225 g (8 oz) carrots, peeled and cut into 5 cm (2 inch) matchsticks
25 g (1 oz) half-fat butter
salt and pepper
chopped fresh parsley and orange segments, to garnish

1 Combine the orange and lemon rind and juice, ginger, hoisin sauce, honey and garlic.
2 Trim the tenderloin of any excess fat. Place in a large shallow non-metallic dish. Pour over the ginger mixture and turn to coat. Cover and marinate in the refrigerator for at least 3–4 hours.
3 Drain the tenderloin. Heat the oil in a large non-stick sauté pan and cook the tenderloin until well browned. Pour over the marinade and chicken stock. Add the carrots. Cover and simmer gently for 15 minutes or until the pork is cooked.
4 Remove the tenderloin with a slotted spoon and slice thickly. Boil the pan juices for 2–3 minutes, until syrupy. Remove from the heat and gradually whisk in the butter. Adjust the seasoning.
5 Return the sliced pork, to the pan, cover and simmer for 1–2 minutes. Garnish with parsley and orange segments and serve.

NOT SUITABLE FOR FREEZING
210 Calories per serving

RATATOUILLE PORK

Preparation time: 8 minutes
Cooking time: 35 minutes

SERVES 4

Pork fillet is ideal for slimmers as it has very little fat, and the fat can be trimmed away easily.

1 aubergine, about 225 g (8 oz)
salt and pepper
30 ml (2 tbsp) olive oil
450 g (1 lb) lean pork fillet, sliced
125 g (4 oz) onion, skinned and chopped
5 ml (1 tsp) dried oregano
1.25 ml (¼ tsp) five-spice powder
225 g (8 oz) courgettes, sliced
400 g (14 oz) can chopped tomatoes
300 ml (½ pint) stock
15 ml (1 tbsp) tomato purée
1 garlic clove, skinned and crushed
about 30 ml (2 tbsp) thickening granules
fresh oregano leaves, to garnish
boiled rice or crusty bread, to serve

1 Halve the aubergine lengthways and slice thickly. Sprinkle with salt and leave for 30 minutes.
2 Heat the oil in a large flameproof casserole, add the pork, onion, oregano and five-spice powder and cook over a high heat, stirring, until the meat is lightly browned.
3 Rinse the aubergine with cold water and drain on absorbent kitchen paper. Add to the casserole with the courgettes, tomatoes, stock, tomato purée, garlic and seasoning.
4 Bring to the boil, cover and cook at 180°C (350°F) mark 4 for 30–35 minutes until the meat and vegetables are tender.
5 Stir in the thickening granules, following the manufacturer's instructions, and season to taste. Garnish with fresh oregano leaves and serve with either boiled rice or crusty bread.

SUITABLE FOR FREEZING
260 Calories per serving

COURGETTE AND BACON RISOTTO

Preparation time: 10 minutes
Cooking time: 25 minutes

SERVES 4

15 ml (1 tbsp) olive oil

125 g (4 oz) onion, skinned and chopped

175 g (6 oz) lean back bacon, derinded and chopped

350 g (12 oz) courgettes, chopped

175 g (6 oz) arborio (risotto) rice

about 800 ml (27 fl oz) chicken stock

75 ml (3 fl oz) dry white wine

grated rind of 1 lemon

2 garlic cloves, skinned and crushed

45 ml (3 tbsp) chopped fresh thyme or parsley

salt and pepper

1 Heat the oil in a shallow, flameproof casserole, preferably non-stick. Add the onion, bacon and courgettes and cook, stirring, over a high heat for 3–4 minutes.

2 Add the rice, most of the stock, wine, lemon rind and garlic. Bring to the boil. Simmer gently, uncovered, for about 20–25 minutes, stirring occasionally until the rice is tender and all the liquid has been absorbed (add a little more stock if necessary). Stir in the thyme, adjust the seasoning and serve.

NOT SUITABLE FOR FREEZING
300 Calories per serving

ABOVE: JAMAICAN JERK LAMB

46

JAMAICAN JERK LAMB

Preparation time: 10 minutes plus marinating
Cooking time: 45 minutes

SERVES 6

15 ml (1 tbsp) olive oil
1 large onion, skinned and finely chopped
2 hot red chillies, deseeded and finely chopped
2 large garlic cloves, skinned and crushed
5 ml (1 tsp) dried thyme
2.5 ml (½ tsp) ground allspice
grated rind and juice of 1 lime
30 ml (2 tbsp) dark rum or Bacardi
salt and pepper
3 fully trimmed racks of lamb, about 700 g (1½ lb) total weight
fine beans and mixed-grain rice, to serve

1 Heat the oil in a saucepan and cook the onion for about 10 minutes or until soft and golden brown. Add the chillies, garlic, dried thyme and allspice. Cook, stirring, for 2–3 minutes.

2 Stir in the lime rind and juice, the rum and 30 ml (2 tbsp) water. Simmer gently, uncovered, for about 4 minutes or until all the liquid has evaporated and the mixture is a dry, dark paste. Season well, then leave to cool.

3 Make about six 1 cm (½ inch) deep cuts at regular intervals along the back of the lamb. Rub the cooled jerk paste into and over the lamb, pressing firmly to coat. Cover and refrigerate overnight.

4 Place the lamb in a roasting tin and cook at 200°C (400°F) mark 6 for 20–25 minutes for medium or 30–35 minutes for well done. Carve into cutlets and serve with fine beans on a bed of mixed rice.

NOT SUITABLE FOR FREEZING
200 Calories per serving

COOK'S TIPS

This dish can be prepared up to 2 days ahead – prepare to the end of step 4 and refrigerate until required.

To give your rice a twist, try one of the following:
Cook the rice with slices of lemon and a pinch of ground turmeric.

Stir in freshly ground black pepper and chopped fresh chives after draining the rice.

Stir in 30–45 ml (2–3 tbsp) low-calorie French dressing.

Toss in crisply fried onion rings and toasted chopped nuts.

LAMB CHOPS WITH LEEKS AND LENTILS

Preparation time: 15 minutes plus marinating
Cooking time: 30 minutes

SERVES 4

4 loin lamb chops, about 125 g (4 oz) each
1 small onion, skinned and finely chopped
125 ml (4 fl oz) fresh orange juice
salt and pepper
450 g (1 lb) trimmed leeks
15 ml (1 tbsp) olive oil
125 g (4 oz) split red lentils
5 ml (1 tsp) ground paprika
300 ml (½ pint) light stock
fresh coriander, to garnish
steamed potatoes, to serve

1 Trim the chops of any excess fat and place in a small, non-metallic dish. Sprinkle the onion over the lamb. Pour over the orange juice and season with black pepper. Cover and refrigerate for at least 12 hours, turning once.
2 Cut the leeks into 1 cm (½ inch) thick slices. Wash in several changes of cold water then drain.
3 Lift the chops out of the marinade and drain on absorbent kitchen paper. Heat the oil in a sauté pan and cook the chops until well browned on both sides. Drain on absorbent kitchen paper.
4 Add the leeks, lentils and paprika to the pan and cook, stirring, over a moderate heat for about 1 minute. Add the chops, marinade and stock and bring to the boil. Cover and simmer for 20 minutes, or until the meat and lentils are quite tender and most of the liquid has been absorbed. Adjust the seasoning, garnish with fresh coriander and serve with steamed potatoes.

NOT SUITABLE FOR FREEZING
390 Calories per serving

INDIAN LAMB WITH SPINACH

Preparation time: 15 minutes plus marinating
Cooking time: 1 hour 10 minutes

SERVES 4

700 g (1½ lb) boned leg or shoulder of lamb
1 cm (½ inch) piece of fresh root ginger, peeled and finely chopped
2 garlic cloves, skinned and crushed
60 ml (4 tbsp) low-fat natural yogurt
2.5 cm (1 inch) cinnamon stick
2 bay leaves
2 green cardamom pods
4 black peppercorns
15 ml (1 tbsp) garam masala
1.25–2.5 ml (¼–½ tsp) chilli powder
salt and pepper
450 g (1 b) fresh spinach or 225 g (8 oz) frozen chopped spinach, thawed
sprigs of mint and lemon slices, to garnish

1 Trim the lamb of fat, cut into small chunks and place in a non-metallic dish. Combine the ginger, garlic, yogurt, cinnamon, bay leaves, cardamoms, peppercorns, garam masala, chilli powder and 5 ml (1 tsp) salt. Stir the spice mixture into the lamb. Cover and leave to marinate at room temperature for about 4 hours.
2 Meanwhile, thoroughly wash and chop the fresh spinach, if using. Drain the frozen spinach.
3 Put the marinated meat in a heavy-based saucepan with the marinade. Bring to the boil and simmer over a low heat for about 1 hour, stirring occasionally, until all the liquid has evaporated and the meat is tender.
4 Stir in the spinach and cook over a low heat for 10 minutes, stirring occasionally. Serve garnished with mint and lemon.

NOT SUITABLE FOR FREEZING
320 Calories per serving

SPICED LAMB WITH POTATOES

Preparation time: 8 minutes
Cooking time: 45 minutes

SERVES 4

450 g (1 lb) lean boneless lamb
30 ml (2 tbsp) seasoned plain flour
30 ml (2 tbsp) olive oil
125 g (4 oz) onion, skinned and chopped
1 red pepper, deseeded and chopped
5 ml (1 tsp) ground ginger
15 ml (1 tbsp) ground coriander
450 ml (¾ pint) stock
15 ml (1 tbsp) soy sauce
15 ml (1 tbsp) Worcestershire sauce
350 g (12 oz) small new potatoes, scrubbed and halved or sliced
50 g (2 oz) black olives (optional)
fresh coriander leaves, to garnish
steamed broccoli, to serve

1 Cut the lamb into small slices and toss in the seasoned flour. Heat the oil in a large flameproof casserole, add the lamb and cook until browned. Remove with a slotted spoon and drain on absorbent kitchen paper.
2 Add the onions and red pepper and sauté for 2 minutes. Add the spices and any remaining flour and cook, stirring, for 1 minute. Stir in the stock, soy sauce and Worcestershire sauce and return the meat to the casserole with the potatoes.
3 Bring to the boil, cover and cook at 180°C (350°F) mark 4 for 40 minutes or until the meat and potatoes are tender.
4 Stir in the olives, if using, and adjust the seasoning. Garnish with coriander leaves and serve with steamed broccoli.

NOT SUITABLE FOR FREEZING
415 Calories per serving

ORIENTAL BEEF STIR-FRY

Preparation time: 20 minutes plus marinating
Cooking time: 10–15 minutes

SERVES 4–6

350 g (12 oz) fillet steak
15 ml (1 tbsp) chilli or stir-fry oil
2 bunches of spring onions, trimmed and cut into 5 cm (2 inch) lengths
2 orange peppers, deseeded and cut into strips
1 hot red chilli, deseeded and cut into fine strips
225 g (8 oz) broccoli, cut into small florets
175 g (6 oz) spinach (or pak choi or choi sam), shredded
noodles, to serve

FOR THE MARINADE
30 ml (2 tbsp) sherry vinegar
30 ml (2 tbsp) black bean sauce
30 ml (2 tbsp) yellow bean sauce
2.5 cm (1 inch) piece of fresh root ginger, peeled and grated
15 ml (1 tbsp) dark soy sauce

1 To make the marinade, mix the sherry vinegar with the black and yellow bean sauces. Add the ginger and the soy sauce.
2 Slice the fillet steak into thin strips about 5 cm (2 inches) wide. Stir into the marinade. Cover and leave to marinate in a cool place for at least 30 minutes or up to 12 hours in the refrigerator.
3 Remove the meat from the marinade with a slotted spoon. Heat the oil in a large non-stick frying pan or wok, add the meat and cook for 3–4 minutes. Add the vegetables. Stir in the marinade and heat through for 3–4 minutes. Serve immediately, with noodles.

NOT SUITABLE FOR FREEZING
200–135 Calories per serving

BEEF IN REDCURRANT AND WINE SAUCE

Preparation time: 10 minutes
Cooking time: 12–25 minutes

SERVES 6

550 g (1¼ lb) beef fillet or boneless venison

salt and pepper

30 ml (2 tbsp) olive oil

3 shallots, skinned and finely chopped

75 g (3 oz) lightly smoked streaky bacon, derinded and chopped

20 pink peppercorns in brine, drained and lightly crushed (optional)

175 ml (6 fl oz) red wine

50 ml (2 fl oz) beef stock

15 ml (1 tbsp) lemon juice

pinch of grated nutmeg

30 ml (2 tbsp) redcurrant jelly

puréed vegetables and green vegetables, to serve

1 Cut the beef into even slices and season. Heat the oil in a large, non-stick sauté pan. Cook the beef over a high heat until well browned. Remove from the pan and keep warm.

2 Add the shallots and bacon to the pan and sauté for 3–4 minutes. Add the peppercorns, wine, stock, lemon juice and nutmeg. Bring to the boil, add the redcurrant jelly and stir until dissolved. Season.

3 Replace the meat, cover the pan and simmer for 2–3 minutes for beef or 12–15 minutes for venison, until the meat is tender. Serve immediately, with vegetables.

NOT SUITABLE FOR FREEZING
230 Calories per serving

COOK'S TIP
Venison is low in fat and makes a good alternative to beef.

BEEF WITH PEPPERS

Preparation time: 10 minutes plus marinating
Cooking time: 1 hour 10 minutes

SERVES 4

450 g (1 lb) stewing beef

30 ml (2 tbsp) olive oil

2 garlic cloves, skinned and crushed

225 g (8 oz) shallots or button onions, skinned

10 ml (2 tsp) plain flour

15 ml (1 tbsp) paprika

pinch of grated nutmeg

salt and pepper

125 g (4 oz) brown cap mushrooms, sliced

350 ml (12 fl oz) beef stock

30 ml (2 tbsp) tomato purée

two 200 g (7 oz) jars peppers in white wine vinegar

creamed potatoes and steamed spinach, to serve

1 Cut the beef into thin strips. Put into a dish with the oil and garlic, cover and marinate for at least 1 hour, preferably overnight.

2 Place the beef and the marinade in a flameproof casserole and sauté until the beef is browned. Stir in the whole onions, flour, paprika, nutmeg and seasoning. Cook, stirring, for 1–2 minutes, then add the mushrooms, stock and tomato purée. Bring to the boil, stirring. Cover and cook at 180°C (350°F) mark 4 for 1 hour, or until tender.

3 Drain the peppers and cut into bite-size pieces. Add to the casserole and return to the oven for 15 minutes. Serve with creamed potatoes and steamed spinach.

SUITABLE FOR FREEZING
250 Calories per serving

COOK'S TIP
If you can't find peppers in white wine vinegar, use those in brine and add 10 ml (2 tsp) vinegar.

COUNTRY BEEF WITH BARLEY

Preparation time: 20 minutes
Cooking time: 2 hours 15 minutes

SERVES 4

450 g (1 lb) stewing beef
25 g (1 oz) seasoned plain flour
15 ml (1 tbsp) olive oil
350 g (12 oz) carrots, peeled and cut into chunks
550 g (1¼ lb) swede, peeled and cut into chunks
2 celery sticks, cut into chunks
salt and pepper
225 g (8 oz) frozen button onions
1 garlic clove, skinned and crushed
50 g (2 oz) pearl barley
pared rind and juice of 1 orange
150 ml (¼ pint) red wine
2 large sprigs of fresh rosemary or 10 ml (2 tsp) dried rosemary
450–600 ml (¾–1 pint) beef stock
fresh rosemary sprigs, to garnish

1 Trim the beef of excess fat and cut the meat into large chunks. Toss the meat in the seasoned flour until evenly coated. Heat the oil in a large flameproof casserole and cook the beef until well browned. Remove with a slotted spoon and drain on absorbent kitchen paper.
2 Lower the heat and then add the chopped vegetables, onions and garlic, with a little more oil, if necessary. Sauté for 4–5 minutes, stirring occasionally. Return the beef to the casserole with the pearl barley, orange rind and juice, wine, rosemary and enough stock to cover.
3 Bring to the boil, stir well, cover and cook at 170°C (325°F) mark 3 for about 2 hours or until the meat is tender. Adjust the seasoning, garnish with rosemary and serve.

NOT SUITABLE FOR FREEZING
330 Calories per serving

SPICED BEEF WITH HORSERADISH

Preparation time: 10 minutes
Cooking time: 2 hours

SERVES 6

1.1 kg (2½ lb) lean stewing beef
15 ml (1 tbsp) olive oil
450 g (1 lb) onions, skinned and sliced
1 garlic clove, skinned and crushed
225 g (8 oz) button mushrooms, wiped
15 ml (1 tbsp) plain flour
2.5 ml (½ tsp) ground ginger
5 ml (1 tsp) medium-hot curry powder
5 ml (1 tsp) dark muscovado sugar
600 ml (1 pint) beef stock
30 ml (2 tbsp) Worcestershire sauce
salt and pepper
30 ml (2 tbsp) creamed horseradish
45 ml (3 tbsp) chopped fresh parsley

1 Trim the beef of any excess fat and cut into 5 cm (2 inch) pieces. Heat the oil in a large flameproof casserole and cook the meat for 2–3 minutes until browned.
2 Lower the heat and add the onions, garlic and mushrooms. Stir in the flour, spices and sugar and cook, stirring, for 1–2 minutes. Add the stock, Worcestershire sauce and seasoning.
3 Bring to the boil, cover and cook at 170°C (325°F) mark 3 for about 2 hours or until the meat is tender.
4 Stir in the creamed horseradish, adjust the seasoning and sprinkle with parsley.

SUITABLE FOR FREEZING AT THE END OF STEP 4
270 Calories per serving

BEEF AND ONION CASSEROLE

Preparation time: 5 minutes
Cooking time: 35 minutes

SERVES 4

Adding a little horseradish brings out the full flavour of the beef in this casserole.

15 ml (1 tbsp) oil
450 g (1 lb) lean rump steak, thinly sliced
225 g (8 oz) frozen baby onions
45 g (1½ oz) packet beef casserole mix
125 g (4 oz) carrots, thinly sliced
15–30 ml (1–2 tbsp) creamed horseradish
1 bay leaf
salt and pepper
creamed potatoes and broccoli, to serve

1 Heat the oil in a small flameproof casserole, add the meat and onions and cook until lightly browned.
2 Combine the casserole mix with 300 ml (½ pint) water and add to the meat with the carrots, horseradish and bay leaf.
3 Bring to the boil, stirring. Cover and bake at 180°C (350°F) mark 4 for 30–35 minutes, until the meat is tender. Adjust the seasoning. Serve with creamed potatoes and broccoli.

NOT SUITABLE FOR FREEZING
265 Calories per serving

CHINESE BEEF SALAD

Preparation time: 15 minutes plus marinating
Cooking time: 15 minutes

SERVES 6

A superb warm salad that's ideal for entertaining. You'll need a large bowl to toss all the ingredients together, or you can spoon the beef mixture on to a bed of salad.

grated rind and juice of 1 orange
2 large garlic cloves, skinned and crushed
60 ml (4 tbsp) rice wine vinegar or cider vinegar
45 ml (3 tbsp) hoisin sauce
15 ml (1 tbsp) runny honey
700 g (1½ lb) rump steak, cut into thin strips
275 g (10 oz) assorted mushrooms, such as brown cap, oyster, shiitake
10 ml (2 tsp) sesame oil
175 g (6 oz) fresh spinach, trimmed and roughly torn
125 g (4 oz) watercress, trimmed and roughly torn
1 small radicchio, trimmed and roughly torn
salt and pepper
30 ml (2 tbsp) chopped fresh chives, to garnish

1 Mix together the orange rind and juice, garlic, rice wine vinegar, hoisin sauce and honey. Add the strips of steak and stir until evenly coated in the marinade. Cover and leave overnight in the refrigerator.
2 Slice any large mushrooms. Drain the beef from the marinade, reserving the marinade. Heat the oil in a wok or large non-stick frying pan and stir-fry the mushrooms for about 4 minutes or until golden brown and tender. Remove with a slotted spoon and keep warm.
3 Stir-fry the beef, in batches, for about 4 minutes or until browned and tender. Return all the beef to the pan with the mushrooms and marinade and bring to the boil. Boil, stirring, for 1 minute.

4 Put the spinach, watercress and radicchio into a bowl. Toss the beef and mushroom mixture into the salad leaves. Adjust the seasoning and serve immediately, garnished with chives.

NOT SUITABLE FOR FREEZING
200 Calories per serving

COOK'S TIP
Packs of mixed mushrooms can be bought in some large supermarkets.

CHICKEN & PUMPKIN CASSEROLE

Preparation time: 20 minutes
Cooking time: 45 minutes
SERVES 4

65 g (2½ oz) sun-dried tomatoes in oil
4 skinless chicken breast fillets, about 125 g (4 oz) each
175 g (6 oz) onions, chopped
4 garlic cloves, skinned and thinly sliced
1 fresh red chilli, deseeded and finely chopped
450 g (1 lb) pumpkin or swede, cubed
400 g (14 oz) can chopped tomatoes
450 ml (15 fl oz) chicken stock
30 ml (2 tbsp) tomato purée
2 bay leaves
pinch of grated nutmeg
salt and pepper
chopped fresh parsley, to garnish

1 Drain the sun-dried tomatoes, reserving the oil. Slice the tomatoes. Heat 30 ml (2 tbsp) of the oil in a large flameproof casserole. Add the chicken breasts and cook for 4–5 minutes on each side until browned. Remove with a slotted spoon and drain on absorbent kitchen paper.
2 Reduce the heat, add the onions, garlic and chilli to the pan and cook for 5 minutes until soft. Add the pumpkin and cook for about 10 minutes, stirring occasionally, until beginning to soften.
3 Add the remaining ingredients, season and bring to the boil. Return the chicken to the pan. Cover and simmer for about 20 minutes, until the chicken is cooked through. Garnish with parsley and serve.

NOT SUITABLE FOR FREEZING
270 Calories per serving

LEMON, CHICKEN AND MUSHROOM RISOTTO

Preparation time: 15 minutes
Cooking time: 30 minutes

SERVES 4

225 g (8 oz) asparagus spears, courgettes or sugar-snap peas

30 ml (2 tbsp) olive oil

175 g (6 oz) onion, skinned and chopped

175 g (6 oz) arborio (risotto) rice

225 g (8 oz) skinless chicken breast fillet or boneless thighs, cut into small pieces

grated rind of 1 lemon

about 600 ml (1 pint) chicken stock

salt and pepper

225 g (8 oz) brown cap mushrooms, wiped and quartered

125 g (4 oz) cooked, peeled prawns

15 ml (1 tbsp) lemon juice

chopped fresh chives, to garnish

1 Trim the asparagus, if using. Cut off the tips and blanch in boiling water for 2–3 minutes. Drain and then keep warm. Cut the asparagus stalks, the courgettes or sugar-snap peas into 1 cm (½ inch) pieces.

2 Heat the oil in a non-stick saucepan. Add the onion and cook for 5–7 minutes until beginning to brown. Add the rice and cook, stirring, for a few seconds.

3 Add the chicken, the lemon rind and almost all of the stock to the pan. Season. Bring to the boil, cover and simmer for 10 minutes.

4 Stir the asparagus stalks, courgettes or sugar-snap peas and mushrooms into the rice, cover and simmer for 10 minutes, stirring occasionally, until the rice is tender and most of the stock has been absorbed.

5 Stir the prawns and lemon juice into the rice and simmer for 1–2 minutes. Adjust the seasoning.

6 Garnish with the reserved asparagus tips, if using, and chopped chives and serve.

NOT SUITABLE FOR FREEZING
350 Calories per serving

COOK'S TIP
The amount of stock needed depends on how much liquid comes out of the mushrooms. The risotto should have a creamy consistency.

BAKED GINGER CHICKEN

Preparation time: 5 minutes plus marinating
Cooking time: 30–40 minutes

SERVES 4

4 skinless chicken breast fillets, about 150 g (5 oz) each

2 slices of lemon, finely chopped

1 cm (½ inch) piece of fresh root ginger, peeled and grated

1 garlic clove, skinned and crushed

10 ml (2 tsp) soy sauce

30 ml (2 tbsp) dry sherry

60 ml (4 tbsp) unsweetened apple juice

1 Arrange the chicken in a single layer in a non-metallic, ovenproof dish.

2 Mix together the remaining ingredients and pour over the chicken. Cover and leave to marinate in the refrigerator overnight.

3 Cover with foil and bake at 200°C (400°F) mark 6, basting occasionally, for 30–40 minutes, or until the chicken is cooked through. Serve.

NOT SUITABLE FOR FREEZING
200 Calories per serving

LEMON, CHICKEN AND MUSHROOM RISOTTO

HOT RED JUNGLE CURRY

Preparation time: 10 minutes
Cooking time: 20 minutes

SERVES 4

If you like more fiery curries, increase the amount of red curry paste a little.

15 ml (1 tbsp) sunflower oil
350 g (12 oz) skinless chicken breast fillets, cut into strips
30 ml (2 tbsp) red curry paste
2.5 cm (1 inch) piece of fresh root ginger, peeled and finely sliced
125 g (4 oz) aubergine, cut into chunks
125 g (4 oz) baby sweetcorn, halved lengthways
75 g (3 oz) green beans, topped and tailed
75 g (3 oz) button or brown cap mushrooms, wiped and halved if necessary
2–3 kaffir lime leaves (optional)
450 ml (¾ pint) chicken stock
30 ml (2 tbsp) fish sauce
grated rind of ½ lime
5 ml (1 tsp) tomato purée
15 ml (1 tbsp) soft brown sugar
pared lime rind, to garnish

1 Heat the oil in a wok or large sauté pan. Add the chicken and cook, stirring, for 5 minutes or until the chicken turns golden brown.
2 Add the red curry paste and cook, stirring, for 1 minute. Add the ginger, vegetables and lime leaves, if using, and stir·until coated in the red curry paste.
3 Add all the remaining ingredients and bring to the boil. Simmer gently for 10–12 minutes or until the chicken and vegetables are just tender. Serve immediately, garnished with pared lime rind.

SUITABLE FOR FREEZING
200 Calories per serving

CHICKEN AND BROCCOLI HOTPOT

Preparation time: 5 minutes
Cooking time: 35 minutes

SERVES 4

The sauce may at first seem quite thick, but it will thin as the juices ooze out of the chicken and vegetables.

15 ml (1 tbsp) sunflower oil
450 g (1 lb) skinless chicken breast fillets, cut into bite-size pieces
34 g (1¼ oz) packet onion sauce mix
600 ml (1 pint) skimmed milk
15 ml (1 tbsp) wholegrain mustard
salt and pepper
225 g (8 oz) broccoli florets
125 g (4 oz) button mushrooms, wiped and halved if necessary
mixed-grain rice and green salad, to serve

1 Heat the oil in a shallow flameproof casserole and cook the chicken over a high heat until browned. Remove with a slotted spoon and drain on absorbent kitchen paper.
2 Make the packet sauce according to the manufacturer's instructions, using the skimmed milk. Whisk in the mustard and season well.
3 Layer all the ingredients into the casserole. Cover and bake at 180°C (350°F) mark 4 for about 30 minutes, or until the chicken is tender. Serve with mixed-grain rice and a crisp green salad.

NOT SUITABLE FOR FREEZING
290 Calories per serving

ORIENTAL CHICKEN PARCELS

Preparation time: 20 minutes plus marinating
Cooking time: 35 minutes

SERVES 4

3 oranges
60 ml (4 tbsp) orange juice
30 ml (2 tbsp) lemon juice
30 ml (2 tbsp) dark soy sauce
30 ml (2 tbsp) yellow bean sauce
15 ml (1 tbsp) dry sherry
15 ml (1 tbsp) sunflower oil
salt and pepper
50 g (2 oz) stem ginger, thinly sliced or 2.5 cm (1 inch) piece of fresh root ginger, peeled and thinly sliced
1 bunch of spring onions, trimmed and cut into 5 cm (2 inch) matchsticks
125 g (4 oz) carrot, peeled and cut into 5 cm (2 inch) matchsticks
4 skinless chicken breast fillets, about 125 g (4 oz) each

1 In a shallow non-metallic dish, mix the finely grated rind of one orange with the orange juice, lemon juice, soy sauce, yellow bean sauce, sherry, oil and seasoning.
2 Lightly slash the chicken breasts all over and add to the marinade with the ginger, spring onions and carrot. Refrigerate overnight.
3 Segment the remaining oranges. Cut four 30.5 cm (12 inch) squares of foil and pull up the edges to make open purses. Divide the chicken and marinade among the foil parcels and top with the orange segments. Pinch the corners of the foil together and place in a roasting tin.
4 Cook at 180°C (350°F) mark 4 for about 35 minutes or until the chicken is tender. Serve the parcels in soup bowls or deep plates.

NOT SUITABLE FOR FREEZING
215 Calories per serving

GOLDEN CHICKEN WITH CASHEW NUTS

Preparation time: 15 minutes plus marinating
Cooking time: 30 minutes

SERVES 4

125 g (4 oz) onion, skinned and chopped
50 g (2 oz) fresh root ginger, peeled and finely chopped
40 g (1½ oz) unsalted cashew nuts
5 ml (1 tsp) ground turmeric
15 ml (1 tbsp) mild curry paste
300 ml (½ pint) low-fat natural yogurt
salt and pepper
8 chicken drumsticks, skinned
rice pilaff with rocket, to serve

1 Place the onion and ginger in a food processor or blender with the cashews, turmeric, curry paste, yogurt and seasoning. Blend until almost smooth.
2 Lightly slash the chicken all over and place in a non-metallic bowl. Pour over the yogurt mixture and stir until the chicken is completely coated. Cover and refrigerate for at least 3 hours, preferably overnight.
3 Place the chicken and the marinade in a large sauté pan with 100 ml (4 fl oz) water. Bring to the boil, cover and simmer for 20–25 minutes or until the chicken is cooked through.
4 Skim off any fat and adjust the seasoning. Serve with a rice pilaff with a few rocket leaves stirred through.

NOT SUITABLE FOR FREEZING
280 Calories per serving

CHICKEN BREASTS WITH APPLE

Preparation time: 15 minutes
Cooking time: 1 hour

SERVES 4

50 g (2 oz) butter
175 g (6 oz) onion, skinned and chopped
2 crisp eating apples, peeled, cored and grated
50 g (2 oz) mature Cheddar cheese, grated
40 g (1½ oz) fresh breadcrumbs
30 ml (2 tbsp) chopped fresh thyme
salt and pepper
4 chicken breast fillets with skin, about 175 g (6 oz) each
75 ml (3 fl oz) apple juice
20 ml (4 tsp) cornflour
300 ml (½ pint) chicken stock
15 ml (1 tbsp) wholegrain mustard
sautéed squash and green beans, to serve

1 Melt 25 g (1 oz) of the butter in a saucepan and sauté the onion until soft. Leave to cool. Add the apples, cheese, breadcrumbs, thyme and seasoning to the onions and mix well.
2 Loosen the skin of the chicken and push the stuffing underneath, pressing it into place. Put in a roasting tin, dot with the remaining butter and season. Pour the apple juice over.
3 Cook at 190°C (375°F) mark 5 for about 50 minutes or until the chicken is cooked through. Remove the chicken from the pan with a slotted spoon and keep warm.
4 Blend the cornflour with 30 ml (2 tbsp) cold water and add to the pan with the stock and mustard. Bring to the boil, stirring, and cook for 2–3 minutes. Season and spoon over the chicken. Serve with squash and green beans.

NOT SUITABLE FOR FREEZING
330 Calories per serving

CHICKEN BREASTS WITH APPLE

ORIENTAL CHICKEN SALAD

Preparation time: about 20 minutes
Cooking time: about 20 minutes

SERVES 4

4 skinless chicken breast fillets, about 125 g (4 oz) each

175 g (6 oz) baby sweetcorn, halved lengthways

125 g (4 oz) beansprouts

15 ml (1 tbsp) sunflower oil

1 small head of Chinese leaves, shredded

1 head of radicchio, shredded

1 bunch of spring onions, trimmed and sliced

15 ml (1 tbsp) sesame seeds, toasted

25 g (1 oz) alfalfa (optional)

FOR THE MARINADE

15 ml (1 tbsp) peeled and finely chopped fresh root ginger

1 large garlic clove, skinned and crushed

200 ml (7 fl oz) orange juice

60 ml (4 tbsp) lemon juice

60 ml (4 tbsp) light soy sauce

60 ml (4 tbsp) sherry

15 ml (1 tbsp) white wine vinegar

5 ml (1 tsp) runny honey

1 Make three shallow cuts in the flesh of each chicken breast and place in a large, shallow non-metallic dish. Mix together the marinade ingredients and pour over the chicken. Cover and refrigerate for at least 3–4 hours.

2 Cook the sweetcorn in boiling, salted water for 5 minutes. Add the beansprouts and cook for a further 30 seconds. Drain and dry on absorbent kitchen paper. Leave to cool.

3 Remove the chicken breasts from the marinade with a slotted spoon, reserving the marinade. Heat the oil in a large non-stick sauté pan and cook the chicken breasts for 10–12 minutes, turning frequently, until browned and cooked through.

4 Add the reserved marinade and simmer to thicken slightly. Adjust the seasoning.

5 Mix together all the salad ingredients and arrange on serving plates. Place the warm chicken breasts on top of the salad, using the marinade as a dressing. Garnish with toasted sesame seeds and alfalfa sprouts, if wished, and serve.

NOT SUITABLE FOR FREEZING
300 Calories per serving

CIDER ROAST POUSSINS

Preparation time: 15 minutes
Cooking time: 55 minutes

SERVES 4

2 poussins, about 450 g (1 lb) each

125 g (4 oz) low-fat soft cheese with garlic and herbs

30 ml (2 tbsp) chopped fresh mixed herbs, eg parsley, chives, thyme etc

300 ml (½ pint) medium-dry cider

300 ml (½ pint) chicken stock

2 crisp eating apples, cored and thickly sliced

25 g (1 oz) low-fat spread

salt and pepper

new potatoes and steamed courgettes, to serve

1 Halve the poussins lengthways. Mix together the soft cheese and herbs. Ease up the skin of the poussins and fill the 'pocket' with the cheese mixture. Secure with wooden cocktail sticks.

2 Place the poussins, skin side uppermost, in a small roasting tin. Pour in the cider and stock. Add the apples, tucking some underneath the birds.

3 Cook at 200°C (400°F) mark 6 for about 50 minutes or until the poussins are golden and cooked through.

4 Remove the birds and apple from the tin. Cover loosely with foil and then keep warm. Strain the cooking juices into a saucepan and boil until reduced by half. Whisk in the low-fat spread. Season to taste.

5 Remove the cocktail sticks. Serve the poussins and apple slices with the juices and new potatoes and steamed courgettes.

NOT SUITABLE FOR FREEZING
285 Calories per serving

COOK'S TIP

The fat in the skin of a chicken or poussin keeps the meat moist without being absorbed by the meat. Either remove the skin before serving, or leave it on the side of the plate.

CHICKEN LIVER SALAD

Preparation time: 5 minutes
Cooking time: 3–4 minutes

SERVES 2

selection of mixed salad leaves
15 ml (1 tbsp) olive oil
225 g (8 oz) frozen chicken livers, thawed and trimmed
15 ml (1 tbsp) chopped fresh sage
30 ml (2 tbsp) balsamic vinegar
salt and pepper

1 Arrange the salad leaves on two serving plates.
2 I leat the oil in a non stick frying pan, add the chicken livers and sage and cook for 2–3 minutes, stirring all the time. Remove with a slotted spoon and place on top of the salad leaves.
3 Add the vinegar to the pan and season with salt and pepper. Heat, stirring well to incorporate all the sediment and juices in the pan, then pour over the salads. Serve at once.

NOT SUITABLE FOR FREEZING
248 Calories per serving

DEVILLED POUSSINS

Preparation time: 10 minutes
Cooking time: 1¼ hours

SERVES 4

This mix could also be spread over a 1.8 kg (4 lb) chicken; allow about 1½ hours cooking time.

125 g (4 oz) low-fat spread
15 ml (1 tbsp) curry paste
1 large lemon
salt and pepper
4 small poussins
150 ml (¼ pint) chicken stock
75 ml (5 tbsp) fromage frais
60 ml (4 tbsp) chopped fresh coriander or parsley
sprigs of fresh herbs, to garnish
steamed vegetables, to serve

1 Beat together the low-fat spread, the curry paste, 15 ml (1 tbsp) of lemon juice and seasoning. Spread over the poussins.
2 Slice the squeezed lemon and place the slices in a roasting tin. Sit the poussins on top and add the stock.
3 Roast at 190°C (375°F) mark 5 for 1–1¼ hours, basting occasionally. Transfer to a serving dish, cover and keep warm.
4 Remove the lemon slices and reserve. Strain the cooking juices into a small saucepan. Add the fromage frais and heat gently, whisking, until evenly blended. Stir in the coriander and adjust the seasoning. Serve the poussins with the sauce, lemon slices and steamed vegetables, garnished with herbs.

NOT SUITABLE FOR FREEZING
260 Calories per serving

CHICKEN BREASTS WITH MUSTARD AND PARMA HAM

Preparation time: 15 minutes
Cooking time: 30 minutes

SERVES 4

4 skinless chicken breast fillets, about 75 g (3 oz) each
75 g (3 oz) reduced-fat soft cheese
15 ml (1 tbsp) wholegrain mustard
8 slices of Parma ham or thinly sliced cooked ham
new potatoes and a green salad, to serve

1 Make a lengthways slit in each chicken breast. Combine the soft cheese and mustard. Stuff the cheese mixture into the slits.
2 Wrap each chicken breast with 2 slices of ham and enclose in a foil parcel. Cook at 190°C (375°F) mark 5 for 30 minutes or until the chicken is cooked through. Serve with potatoes and a green salad.

NOT SUITABLE FOR FREEZING
175 Calories per serving

VARIATIONS
Omit the mustard and add 25 g (1 oz) chopped sun-dried tomatoes and 25 g (1 oz) chopped black olives to the soft cheese. (This adds an extra 30 calories per serving.)
Heat 15 g (½ oz) butter in a non-stick saucepan and cook 275 g (10 oz) sliced mushrooms, 1 crushed garlic clove and 10 ml (2 tsp) lemon juice until all the liquid has evaporated. Leave to cool. Place in a food processor with 75 g (3 oz) reduced-fat soft cheese and blend until smooth. Use to stuff the chicken breasts. Wrap with ham and cook as above. (This adds an extra 40 calories per serving).

WINTER CHICKEN

Preparation time: 20 minutes
Cooking time: 45 minutes

SERVES 4

4 chicken leg portions, about 700 g (1½ lb) total weight, skinned
15 ml (1 tbsp) seasoned plain flour
15 ml (1 tbsp) olive oil
225 g (8 oz) onion, skinned and cut into chunks
450 g (1 lb) carrots, peeled and cut into chunks
450 g (1 lb) celery, cut into chunks
50 g (2 oz) lean back bacon, derinded, trimmed and chopped
200 ml (7 fl oz) apple juice
400 g (14 oz) can butter beans, drained
1 bunch of watercress, chopped
15–30 ml (2–3 tbsp) lemon juice
salt and pepper

1 Cut the chicken portions into thighs and drumsticks. Toss in seasoned flour.
2 Heat the oil in a flameproof casserole. Add the onion, carrots, celery and bacon and cook for 2–3 minutes. Stir in the apple juice, butter beans and the chicken.
3 Bring to the boil, cover and cook at 180°C (350°F) mark 4 for about 45 minutes or until the chicken is cooked through and all the ingredients are tender.
4 Stir the watercress, lemon juice and seasoning into the casserole. Heat gently to warm through and serve.

NOT SUITABLE FOR FREEZING
350 Calories per serving

CHICKEN BREASTS WITH MUSTARD AND PARMA HAM

CHICKEN WITH MUSTARD SAUCE

Preparation time: 10 minutes
Cooking time: 30 minutes

SERVES 4

20 ml (4 tsp) wholegrain mustard
4 chicken breasts, about 175 g (6 oz) each, skinned
juice of 1 small orange
150 ml (¼ pint) chicken stock
150 ml (¼ pint) low-fat natural yogurt
watercress sprigs, to garnish

1 Spread the mustard over the chicken breasts and place in a flameproof casserole. Sprinkle over the orange juice and stock.
2 Bring to the boil, cover with foil and the lid and simmer for 20–25 minutes or until tender and cooked through.
3 Remove the chicken with a slotted spoon and arrange on warmed serving plates. Keep warm. Add the yogurt to the casserole and mix with any juices and excess mustard from the base of the pan. Heat gently without boiling, stirring constantly, then pour over the chicken. Garnish with sprigs of watercress and serve.

NOT SUITABLE FOR FREEZING
230 Calories per serving

WARM CHICKEN AND WHEAT SALAD

Preparation time: 20 minutes plus marinating
Cooking time: 10 minutes

SERVES 4

30 ml (2 tbsp) mango chutney
45 ml (3 tbsp) lemon or lime juice
30 ml (2 tbsp) sunflower oil
10 ml (2 tsp) garam masala or mild curry powder
5 ml (1 tsp) paprika
salt and pepper
350 g (12 oz) skinless chicken breast fillets, cut into thick strips
125 g (4 oz) bulghur wheat
1 cucumber
1 bunch of spring onions, trimmed and sliced
25 g (1 oz) no-soak dried apricots, sliced
30 ml (2 tbsp) chopped fresh mint
60 ml (4 tbsp) low-fat natural yogurt
15 ml (1 tbsp) shredded fresh mint leaves

1 In a shallow, non-metallic dish, mix together the mango chutney, lemon juice, oil, garam masala, paprika and seasoning. Stir in the chicken. Cover and refrigerate for at least 1 hour, preferably overnight.
2 Place the bulghur wheat in a bowl, pour over 200 ml (7 fl oz) boiling water and leave to soak for about 30 minutes or until all the liquid has been absorbed (follow the packet instructions as some bulghur wheat takes longer to soften). Meanwhile, halve the cucumber lengthways, scoop out the seeds and roughly chop the flesh. Put in a nylon sieve, sprinkle with salt and leave for about 30 minutes. Rinse and drain well.
3 Mix the bulghur wheat with the cucumber, spring onions, apricots, chopped mint and seasoning. Spoon onto a serving dish.
4 Heat a non-stick frying pan, add the chicken and marinade and cook over a high heat for 2–3 minutes, stirring frequently. Pour in 150 ml (¼ pint) water; bring to the boil and cook, uncovered, for

about 5 minutes or until the chicken is tender and the sauce reduced to a coating consistency.

5 Combine the yogurt and shredded mint. Spoon the warm chicken and sauce on to the bulghur wheat salad and serve with the mint yogurt.

NOT SUITABLE FOR FREEZING
340 Calories per serving

COOK'S TIP

Bulghur wheat is cracked grains of wheat which have been partially processed. It only needs to be soaked in boiling water to become tender. Bulghur wheat is very popular in the Middle East, where it is often served cold, in salads.

CHICKEN IN SMOKY BACON SAUCE

Preparation time: 10 minutes
Cooking time: 20 minutes

SERVES 4

30 ml (2 tbsp) sunflower oil

125 g (4 oz) thin-cut smoked streaky bacon, derinded and chopped

4 skinless chicken supremes or breast fillets, about 150 g (5 oz) each

200 ml (7 fl oz) apple juice

15 ml (1 tbsp) chopped fresh thyme or 5 ml (1 tsp) dried thyme

salt and pepper

1 bunch of spring onions, trimmed and chopped

225 g (8 oz) crisp red eating apples, cored and thickly sliced

60 ml (4 tbsp) crème fraîche

noodles or pasta, to serve

1 Heat the oil in a large, deep, frying pan or sauté pan. Add the chopped bacon and chicken supremes and fry for a few minutes until golden, stirring and turning occasionally.

2 Stir in the apple juice, thyme and seasoning. Bring to the boil, cover and simmer gently for 10 minutes.

3 Uncover, then add the chopped spring onions and apples and cook over a high heat for about 5 minutes or until the liquid has reduced by half and the chicken is cooked through.

4 Lower the heat and stir in the crème fraîche. Adjust the seasoning and serve with pasta or noodles.

NOT SUITABLE FOR FREEZING
350 Calories per serving

WARM DUCK SALAD

Preparation time: 10 minutes
Cooking time: 15–20 minutes

SERVES 8

30 ml (2 tbsp) ground coriander
10 ml (2 tsp) ground ginger
10 ml (2 tsp) ground mace
1 garlic clove, skinned and crushed
30 ml (2 tbsp) fresh orange juice
30 ml (2 tbsp) olive oil
salt and pepper
8 boned duck breasts, about 125 g (4 oz) each, skinned
selection of mixed salad leaves
about 20 pitted black olives
FOR THE DRESSING
45 ml (3 tbsp) fresh orange juice
45 ml (3 tbsp) olive oil
7.5 ml (½ tbsp) runny honey
15 ml (1 tbsp) red wine vinegar
7.5 ml (½ tbsp) Dijon mustard

1 Mix together the coriander, ginger, mace and garlic with the orange juice and oil. Season.
2 Spread the spice mixture on both sides of the duck breasts and place in a shallow ovenproof dish. Roast at 200°C (400°F) mark 6 for 15–20 minutes until the duck is tender and browned.
3 Meanwhile, to make the dressing, whisk together the orange juice, oil, honey, vinegar and mustard. Season to taste.
4 Arrange the salad leaves on a shallow serving plate. Remove the duck breasts from the dish with a slotted spoon, slice neatly and arrange on the salad leaves. Scatter over the olives, spoon over the dressing and serve.

NOT SUITABLE FOR FREEZING
327 Calories per serving

CHICKEN BAKED WITH SPICES

Preparation time: 15 minutes plus marinating
Cooking time: 25 minutes

SERVES 6

2 garlic cloves, skinned and crushed
30 ml (2 tbsp) mild paprika
10 ml (2 tsp) ground coriander
5–10 ml (1–2 tsp) cayenne pepper
finely grated rind and juice of 1 large lemon
30 ml (2 tbsp) chopped fresh mint
30 ml (2 tbsp) chopped fresh coriander
45 ml (3 tbsp) grated fresh coconut (optional)
200 ml (7 fl oz) thick yogurt
salt and pepper
6 chicken supremes, or other portions, skinned
melted butter or vegetable oil for brushing
lemon or lime wedges, to garnish

1 Mix the garlic with the paprika, coriander, cayenne pepper and lemon rind and juice. Put the herbs and coconut, if using, in a large, shallow non-metallic dish and stir in the yogurt. Beat in the garlic mixture. Add salt and pepper to taste.
2 Make 2 or 3 deep cuts in the thickest part of the chicken. Place the chicken portions in the yogurt mixture and turn to coat, making sure that the marinade goes well into the slashes. Leave to marinate in a cool place for at least 30 minutes or overnight if possible.
3 Arrange the chicken in a single layer in a roasting tin and brush with melted butter or oil. Roast at 200°C (400°F) mark 6, basting from time to time, for about 25 minutes until the chicken is cooked through. Garnish with lemon or lime wedges and serve.

NOT SUITABLE FOR FREEZING
260 Calories per serving

THAI CHICKEN SALAD

Preparation time: 20 minutes plus marinating
Cooking time: 20 minutes

SERVES 6

450 g (1 lb) skinless chicken breast fillets, cut into thin strips

5 ml (1 tsp) caster sugar

2.5 ml (½ tsp) each salt, pepper, ground ginger, mustard powder, turmeric and medium curry powder

60 ml (4 tbsp) olive oil

350 g (12 oz) courgettes, sliced

150 g (5 oz) mangetout, trimmed

1 each red and yellow pepper, deseeded and cut into strips

45 ml (3 tbsp) runny honey

60 ml (4 tbsp) lemon juice

2.5 cm (1 inch) piece of fresh root ginger, peeled and finely chopped

250 g (9 oz) medium egg noodles

50 g (2 oz) salted cashew nuts

1 Mix the chicken with the sugar, salt, pepper and spices. Cover and refrigerate overnight.

2 Heat half the oil in a frying pan and sauté the courgettes for 2–3 minutes. Remove with a slotted spoon and transfer to a large bowl. Add the mangetout and peppers to the pan and sauté for 2–3 minutes. Add to the courgettes.

3 Heat the remaining oil and sauté the chicken, in batches, until golden brown. Return all the chicken to the pan and stir in the honey, lemon juice and ginger. Cover and simmer for about 5 minutes or until the chicken is quite tender.

4 Break the noodles into smaller pieces and cook according to the packet instructions. Drain and mix with the chicken and vegetables. Season. Sprinkle with the nuts and serve warm or cold.

NOT SUITABLE FOR FREEZING
415 Calories per serving

LEMON CHICKEN KEBABS

Preparation time: 10–15 minutes
Cooking time: 20 minutes

SERVES 4

juice of 1 lemon

15 ml (1 tbsp) olive oil

1 garlic clove, skinned and crushed

salt and pepper

8 boned and skinned chicken thighs, about 350 g (12 oz) total weight

1 small red pepper, deseeded and cut into bite-size pieces

225 g (8 oz) small courgettes, thickly sliced

1 green eating apple, cored and thickly sliced

450 g (1 lb) leeks, trimmed and shredded

25 g (1 oz) butter or margarine

1 Mix together the lemon juice, oil, garlic and seasoning. Cut each chicken thigh in half and place in the lemon mixture. Stir and leave to marinate for about 15 minutes.

2 Thread the chicken, pepper, courgettes and apple on to skewers and brush with the lemon marinade. Grill for 15–20 minutes, turning and basting with the marinade.

3 Meanwhile, put the leeks in a saucepan with the butter or margarine and 30 ml (2 tbsp) water. Cover and simmer for about 15 minutes or until tender. Season with plenty of black pepper.

4 Serve the kebabs on a bed of leeks.

NOT SUITABLE FOR FREEZING
280 Calories per serving

CHICKEN HOT POT

Preparation time: 15 minutes
Cooking time: 1 hour 35 minutes

SERVES 4

15 ml (1 tbsp) sunflower oil

1 large garlic clove, skinned and crushed

700 g (1½ lb) trimmed leeks, thickly sliced

200 g (7 oz) reduced-fat soft cheese with garlic and herbs

100 ml (4 fl oz) white wine

175 ml (6 fl oz) chicken stock

10 ml (2 tsp) cornflour

8 skinless, boneless chicken thighs, about 350 g (12 oz) total weight

salt and pepper

275 g (10 oz) unpeeled potatoes, thinly sliced

1 Heat the oil in a flameproof casserole. Add the garlic and leeks and cook for about 5 minutes or until beginning to soften.

2 Meanwhile place the cheese, wine, stock and cornflour in a food processor or blender and purée until smooth.

3 Arrange the chicken thighs on top of the leeks, pour over the cheese mixture and season to taste. Layer the potatoes on top of the chicken. Place a lightly oiled sheet of baking parchment on top of the potatoes, then cover the casserole with a lid or foil.

4 Cook at 180°C (350°F) mark 4 for 1½ hours or until the potatoes are quite tender. Brown the potatoes under a hot grill before serving.

NOT SUITABLE FOR FREEZING
350 Calories per serving

TURKEY AND CUCUMBER SAUTÉ

Preparation time: 5 minutes
Cooking time: 12 minutes

SERVES 4

4 small turkey escalopes, about 125 g (4 oz) each

250 ml (9 fl oz) chicken stock

125 ml (4 fl oz) dry vermouth

30 cm (12 inch) piece of cucumber, peeled and sliced

50 g (2 oz) half-fat butter

20 ml (4 tbsp) plain flour

5 ml (1 tsp) wholegrain mustard

salt and pepper

15 ml (1 tbsp) chopped fresh chives

toasted split cashew nuts, to garnish

1 Put the turkey in a single layer in a frying pan. Add the stock and vermouth, cover and poach for 5 minutes.

2 Add the cucumber to the pan and cook for a further 5 minutes.

3 Mix together the half-fat butter, flour and mustard. Remove the turkey and cucumber from the pan with a slotted spoon and keep warm.

4 Whisk the butter mixture into the juices in the pan. Bring to the boil and simmer very gently for 1–2 minutes, stirring. Adjust the seasoning. Return the turkey, cucumber and any juice to the pan, add the chives and heat gently to warm through. Scatter with the nuts and serve.

NOT SUITABLE FOR FREEZING
230 Calories per serving

CHICKEN HOT POT

TURKEY ENCHILADAS

Preparation time: 20 minutes
Cooking time: 25 minutes

SERVES 4

450 g (1 lb) skinless turkey breast fillets, cut into small dice

5 ml (1 tsp) ground cumin

10 ml (2 tsp) vegetable oil

1 red onion, skinned and finely chopped

1 red pepper, deseeded and finely chopped

2.5 ml (½ tsp) each ground cinnamon, ground ginger and dried thyme

5 pitted green olives, chopped

15 ml (1 tbsp) capers, chopped

25 g (1 oz) raisins

400 g (14 oz) can chopped tomatoes

salt and pepper

4 flour tortillas (see Cook's Tips)

250 g (9 oz) passata (see Cook's Tips)

25 g (1 oz) grated cheese, such as mozzarella or low-fat Cheddar

30 ml (2 tbsp) chopped fresh chives

150 g (5 oz) low-fat natural fromage frais

fresh flat-leaf parsley, to garnish

1 Toss the turkey in the ground cumin. Heat half the oil in a non-stick frying pan and cook the turkey for about 8 minutes or until golden brown and cooked through. Set aside.

2 Heat the remaining oil and fry the onion and the red pepper for 5 minutes or until soft. Add the cinnamon, ginger and thyme and cook, stirring, for 30 seconds. Stir in the olives, capers, raisins and chopped tomatoes. Simmer gently for 8 minutes or until thick and reduced by half. Stir in the cooked turkey and season well.

3 Divide the mixture among the flour tortillas, fold over and secure with wooden satay or cocktail sticks. Place the tortillas on to heatproof serving plates. Spread the passata over the tortillas, sprinkle with the grated cheese and cook under a

hot grill for 3–4 minutes or until the cheese is bubbling and golden brown.

4 While the tortillas are browning, mix together the chives and fromage frais. Season well. Garnish the tortillas with flat-leaf parsley, top with a spoonful of creamy chive sauce and serve.

NOT SUITABLE FOR FREEZING
345 Calories per serving

COOK'S TIPS
Flour tortillas are now available in most major supermarkets. If you're unable to find them, make thin crêpes using a pancake batter made with skimmed milk.
Passata is a thick tomato sauce made from puréed and sieved tomatoes and is available in bottles or cartons from most major supermarkets.

TROPICAL CHICKEN SALAD

Preparation time: 20 minutes plus chilling
Cooking time: 15–20 minutes

SERVES 6

2.5 cm (1 inch) piece fresh root ginger, peeled and finely chopped

1 fresh red chilli, deseeded and finely chopped

45 ml (3 tbsp) runny honey

1 garlic clove, skinned and crushed

5 ml (1 tsp) mixed spice

700 g (1½ lb) skinless chicken breast fillets, cut into strips

200 g (7 oz) crème fraîche

30 ml (2 tbsp) mayonnaise

juice of 3 limes

salt and pepper

1 bunch of spring onions, chopped

900 g (2 lb) mixed tropical fruits, such as mango, pawpaw, melon, pineapple or kiwi fruit

2 ripe avocados
45 ml (3 tbsp) chopped fresh coriander
chopped spring onions and coriander sprigs, to garnish

1 Mix together the ginger, chilli, honey, garlic and mixed spice. Put the chicken in a shallow ovenproof dish, add the honey mixture and toss to coat. Cover and refrigerate for 30 minutes.
2 Uncover and cook at 190°C (375°F) mark 5 for 15–20 minutes, until the chicken is cooked through. Leave to cool in the liquid, then drain.
3 Mix together the crème fraîche, mayonnaise, a third of the lime juice and seasoning.
4 Mix the chicken with the crème fraîche mixture and the spring onions. Cut the fruits into bite-size pieces. Peel the avocados and cut the flesh into bite-size pieces. Mix the remaining lime juice with the coriander and toss with the fruits and avocados.
5 Pile the chicken into the centre of a serving dish and surround with the fruit mixture. Garnish with spring onions and coriander and serve.

NOT SUITABLE FOR FREEZING
330 Calories per serving

COOK'S TIP
For a spicier dish, leave the seeds in the chilli.

GREEN CHICKEN CURRY

Preparation time: 30 minutes plus standing
Cooking time: 30 minutes

SERVES 4

4 baby aubergines, quartered
5 ml (1 tsp) sea salt
30 ml (2 tbsp) sunflower oil

4 shallots, skinned and halved or quartered
2 garlic cloves, skinned and sliced
30 ml (2 tbsp) green curry paste
150 ml (¼ pint) chicken stock
15 ml (1 tbsp) Thai fish sauce
15 ml (1 tbsp) lemon juice
350 g (12 oz) skinless chicken breast fillets, cubed
1 red pepper, deseeded and sliced
125 g (4 oz) French beans, trimmed and halved
25 g (1 oz) creamed coconut, grated
rice, to serve

1 Put the aubergines in a colander, sprinkle with the salt and leave for 30 minutes. Rinse well in cold water and pat dry with absorbent kitchen paper.
2 Heat the oil in a large frying pan, add the shallots and garlic and cook for 3 minutes until lightly browned. Add the green curry paste and cook, stirring, for 2–3 minutes.
3 Stir in the stock, fish sauce and lemon juice. Bring to the boil and simmer for 10 minutes.
4 Add the chicken, red pepper, French beans and aubergines to the pan and return to the boil. Simmer for 10–15 minutes until the chicken and vegetables are tender.
5 Add the creamed coconut and heat gently, stirring, until the coconut is melted and the sauce is thickened – do not boil. Serve with rice.

NOT SUITABLE FOR FREEZING
255 Calories per serving

VEGETABLE ACCOMPANIMENTS AND SALADS

VEGETABLE AND APPLE STIR-FRY

Preparation time: 15 minutes
Cooking time: 15 minutes

SERVES 4

60 ml (4 tbsp) vegetable oil
1 garlic clove, skinned and crushed
350 g (12 oz) small leeks, trimmed and sliced
4 green celery sticks, sliced
225 g (8 oz) courgettes, sliced
1 red pepper, deseeded and chopped
30 ml (2 tbsp) medium curry paste
5 ml (1 tsp) ground ginger
15 ml (1 tbsp) runny honey
2 crisp, green eating apples, cored and chopped
50 g (2 oz) unsalted cashew nuts
salt and pepper
1 lemon
flat-leaf parsley, to garnish

1 Heat the oil in a non-stick sauté pan and cook the garlic for a few seconds. Stir in the vegetables and cook over a high heat for 10 minutes, stirring occasionally.

2 Add the curry paste, ginger, honey and 45 ml (3 tbsp) water and stir until smooth.

3 Add the apples to the pan with the cashew nuts and seasoning. Cook for a further 5 minutes or until the vegetables are just tender but retain some bite. Squeeze lemon juice over, garnish with flat-leaf parsley and serve.

NOT SUITABLE FOR FREEZING
285 Calories per serving

COOK'S TIP
To prepare ahead, prepare the vegetables as in step 1 and store in the refrigerator in polythene bags for up to 12 hours.

VEGETABLE AND APPLE STIR-FRY

YELLOW SPLIT PEAS WITH COCONUT

Preparation time: 5 minutes
Cooking time: about 30 minutes

SERVES 6

275 g (10 oz) yellow split peas
75 g (3 oz) creamed coconut, grated
60 ml (4 tbsp) single cream, optional
salt and pepper
chopped fresh coriander, to garnish

1 Cook the split peas in a saucepan of boiling salted water for 30–35 minutes, or until just tender.
2 Drain the peas and return to the pan. Add the coconut and stir until melted throughout. Add the cream, if using, and seasoning. Garnish with coriander and serve.

NOT SUITABLE FOR FREEZING
200 Calories per serving

SPICY MUSHROOMS

Preparation time: 15 minutes
Cooking time: 40 minutes

SERVES 6

60–75 ml (4–5 tbsp) olive oil
350 g (12 oz) aubergine, cut into chunks
3 garlic cloves, skinned and crushed
450 g (1 lb) onions, finely sliced
5 cm (2 inch) piece fresh root ginger, peeled and grated
10 ml (2 tsp) hot chilli powder
5 ml (1 tsp) turmeric
5 ml (1 tsp) garam masala
5 ml (1 tsp) ground cumin
two 400 g (14 oz) cans chopped tomatoes
salt and pepper
350 g (12 oz) button mushrooms, wiped and halved
225 g (8 oz) frozen peas

1 Heat 60 ml (4 tbsp) oil in a large, non-stick frying pan and fry the aubergine pieces until golden brown, adding more oil if necessary. Remove the aubergine from the pan and drain on absorbent kitchen paper.
2 Add a little more oil to the pan if necessary then add the garlic, onions and ginger. Cook until golden, stirring occasionally. Add the spices and cook for 1 minute, stirring all the time.
3 Return the aubergine to the pan with the tomatoes and seasoning. Bring to the boil, cover and simmer for about 20 minutes or until the aubergines are tender.
4 Stir in the mushrooms and frozen peas and cook for about 10 minutes, adding a little water if necessary to thin the sauce slightly. Serve.

NOT SUITABLE FOR FREEZING
150 Calories per serving

PURÉED VEGETABLES

Preparation time: 15 minutes
Cooking time: 25 minutes

SERVES 6

**450 g (1 lb) each potatoes, parsnips and carrots,
or other root vegetables**
1.1 litres (2 pints) vegetable or chicken stock
300 ml (½ pint) very low-fat fromage frais
25 g (1 oz) low-fat spread
salt and pepper
chopped fresh chives, to garnish

1 Peel the potatoes, parsnips and carrots and
roughly chop into even-size pieces. Bring the
stock to the boil in a large saucepan, add the
vegetables, cover and cook for about 20 minutes.
2 Drain and place in a food processor or blender
with the fromage frais. Purée until smooth.
3 Return to a clean saucepan with the low-fat
spread. Stir over a moderate heat until hot.
Season, garnish with chives and serve.

SUITABLE FOR FREEZING
165 Calories per serving

BAKED VEGETABLE PURSES

Preparation time: 10 minutes
Cooking time: 35–45 minutes

SERVES 6

This recipe is simple to prepare and the baby
vegetables look lovely in the little purses. Ordinary-
size vegetables, cut into bite-size pieces, work
equally well.

**900 g (2 lb) mixed baby vegetables, eg carrots,
turnips, fennel, parsnips and button onions**
50 g (2 oz) butter
4 garlic cloves, skinned and crushed
75 ml (3 fl oz) vegetable stock
75 ml (3 fl oz) orange juice
15 ml (1 tbsp) runny honey
5 ml (1 tsp) dried thyme
salt and pepper

1 Cut out six 30.5 cm (12 inch) squares of foil.
Skin the onions and halve if necessary.
2 Melt the butter in a frying pan and stir-fry the
vegetables for about 3 minutes or until beginning
to brown. Divide equally among the squares of
foil, pulling the edges up to make open purses.
3 Add the garlic and remaining ingredients to the
pan and simmer for 2 minutes. Season. Pour over
the vegetables and close the purses tightly. Stand
the purses on a baking sheet.
4 Roast at 220°C (425°F) mark 7 for 30–40
minutes or until just tender. Serve the vegetables
still wrapped in the foil.

NOT SUITABLE FOR FREEZING
110 Calories per serving

COOK'S TIP
The turnips and carrots take the longest to cook,
so test carefully with the point of a sharp knife and
return to the oven for a little longer if necessary.

STEAMED COUSCOUS AND WATERCRESS

Preparation time: 10 minutes
Cooking time: 35 minutes

SERVES 6

175 g (6 oz) couscous
25 g (1 oz) brown rice, cooked
75 g (3 oz) melted butter
salt and pepper
1 bunch of watercress, chopped

1 Cover the couscous with 300 ml (½ pint) cold water. Leave for 10 minutes or until all the water is absorbed. Add the rice, butter and seasoning.
2 Spoon the couscous mixture into a wire sieve or metal colander lined with muslin or a J-cloth. Put over a pan of boiling water and cover with foil. Steam for about 35 minutes until the couscous is tender. Stir in the watercress. Adjust the seasoning and serve.

NOT SUITABLE FOR FREEZING
165 Calories per serving

STIR-FRIED BROCCOLI

Preparation time: 5 minutes
Cooking time: 6–8 minutes

SERVES 6

30 ml (2 tbsp) red wine vinegar
30 ml (2 tbsp) soy sauce
15 ml (1 tbsp) sesame oil
10 ml (2 tsp) cornflour
5 ml (1 tsp) caster sugar
900 g (2 lb) broccoli
½ head of crisp lettuce, eg cos
45 ml (3 tbsp) vegetable oil

1 garlic clove, skinned and crushed
30 ml (2 tbsp) sesame seeds
salt and pepper

1 Whisk together the first five ingredients in a large bowl. Cut the broccoli into medium florets, discarding the coarse stalks. Cook the broccoli in a saucepan of boiling salted water for 2–3 minutes. Drain and toss into the soy sauce mixture. Roughly chop the lettuce.
2 Heat the vegetable oil in a wok or large frying pan. Add all the ingredients and stir-fry for 4–5 minutes. Season and serve.

NOT SUITABLE FOR FREEZING
160 Calories per serving

GREEN BEANS WITH CUMIN

Preparation time: 10 minutes
Cooking time: 20 minutes

SERVES 6

45 ml (3 tbsp) olive oil
125 g (4 oz) onions, sliced
700 g (1½ lb) green beans, topped and tailed and halved
10 ml (2 tsp) cumin seeds
450 g (1 lb) tomatoes, peeled and chopped
30 ml (2 tbsp) tomato purée
salt and pepper

1 Heat the oil in a large sauté pan. Add the onions and cook, stirring, for 1–2 minutes. Add the beans and cumin seeds and cook, stirring, for a further 2–3 minutes.
2 Stir in the tomatoes, tomato purée and 150 ml (¼ pint) water. Season. Bring to the boil, cover and simmer for 15 minutes or until the beans are just tender. Adjust the seasoning and serve.

NOT SUITABLE FOR FREEZING
80 Calories per serving

ROASTED VEGETABLE SALAD

Preparation time: 15 minutes
Cooking time: 45 minutes

SERVES 4

225 g (8 oz) aubergine, cut into chunks
350 g (12 oz) courgette, cut into chunks
1 red pepper, deseeded and quartered
1 yellow pepper, deseeded and quartered
225 g (8 oz) tomatoes, halved
6 garlic cloves, skinned
75 ml (5 tbsp) olive oil
rock salt and milled black pepper
1 lemon

1 Place all the vegetables in a large roasting tin in a single layer. Sprinkle over the olive oil and season generously with plenty of rock salt.
2 Roast at 200°C (400°F) mark 6 for about 45 minutes or until the vegetables are tender and well browned, turning once during cooking.
3 Leave in the tin to cool for 30 minutes, then squeeze lemon juice over to taste and adjust the seasoning. Lift the vegetables on to serving plates or into one large bowl. Serve immediately or leave to cool completely.

NOT SUITABLE FOR FREEZING
215 Calories per serving

COOK'S TIP
To make a complete meal with this salad, thickly slice a crusty loaf and rub each slice with a garlic clove. Toast lightly on both sides. Spread the toast thickly on one side with pesto sauce or tapénade (olive paste), then top with slices of mozzarella, Emmental or goat's cheese. Grill again until the cheese just begins to melt.

ROASTED VEGETABLE SALAD

SALADE NIÇOISE

Preparation time: 15 minutes
Cooking time: 20 minutes

SERVES 4

This salad is delicious whether the vegetables are hot or cold (if you are serving them cold, cool them before tossing).

450 g (1 lb) small new potatoes
125 g (4 oz) French beans, topped and tailed
4 ripe tomatoes, chopped
2 hard-boiled eggs, cut into wedges
50 g (2 oz) pitted black olives
200 g (7 oz) can tuna in brine, drained
15 g (½ oz) canned anchovies, drained
30 ml (2 tbsp) olive oil
15 ml (1 tbsp) white wine vinegar
pinch of sugar
pinch of mustard powder
5 ml (1 tsp) lemon juice
salt and pepper
mixed salad leaves, to serve

1 Put the potatoes in a saucepan of salted water and bring to the boil. Cook for 15–20 minutes, or until tender. Cook the French beans in a saucepan of boiling salted water for 3 minutes, or until just tender.
2 Toss together the potatoes, beans, tomatoes, eggs, olives and tuna and top with the anchovies.
3 Whisk together the remaining ingredients. Season to taste. Pile the vegetable mixture on to a bed of mixed salad leaves and pour over the dressing.

NOT SUITABLE FOR FREEZING
225 Calories per serving with dressing
165 Calories per serving without dressing

CARROT SALAD WITH ORANGE AND HONEY DRESSING

Preparation time: 15 minutes
Cooking time: nil

SERVES 4

To make this a more substantial meal, add 25 g (1 oz) peanuts.

2 oranges
450 g (1 lb) carrots, coarsely grated
15 ml (1 tbsp) poppy seeds
90 ml (6 tbsp) fresh orange juice
1 small garlic clove, skinned and crushed
2.5 ml (½ tsp) balsamic vinegar
5 ml (1 tsp) runny honey
30 ml (2 tbsp) chopped fresh chives
salt and pepper

1 Cut the top and bottom off each orange. Remove the skin with a serrated knife, taking care to remove all the pith. Thinly slice the oranges.
2 Mix together the carrots, sliced oranges and poppy seeds in a large bowl.
3 Whisk together the orange juice, garlic, vinegar and honey. Stir in the chopped chives and seasoning.
4 Just before serving, pour the dressing over the salad and gently toss.

NOT SUITABLE FOR FREEZING
55 Calories per serving

CRISP VEGETABLE SALAD

Preparation time: 20 minutes
Cooking time: 5 minutes

SERVES 6

Instead of offering the usual green salad as part of a summer buffet, try this mix of crisp vegetables. It's easy to prepare all the vegetables the day before and keep them chilled, leaving them ready to dress when required.

450 g (1 lb) broccoli
225 g (8 oz) asparagus
150 g (5 oz) mangetout
450 g (1 lb) fennel
90 ml (6 tbsp) olive oil
30 ml (2 tbsp) white wine vinegar
5 ml (1 tsp) Dijon mustard
pinch of sugar
salt and pepper

1 Trim the broccoli into bite-sized florets. Cut off the asparagus tips and cut the stalks into 2.5 cm (1 inch) pieces. Top and tail the mangetout and cut the fennel into large chunks, reserving the feathery tops for the dressing.
2 Plunge the asparagus and mangetout into a saucepan of boiling salted water and boil for 1 minute. Meanwhile, fill a basin with cold water and add some ice cubes.
3 Remove the asparagus and the mangetout from the pan with a slotted spoon or fish slice and plunge into the cold water. Leave for 1 minute. Lift the vegetables out of the water and drain well on absorbent kitchen paper.
4 Add the broccoli and fennel to the pan and simmer for 3 minutes. Transfer to the cold water and leave for 2–3 minutes. Drain well. Toss the vegetables together. Cover and refrigerate.
5 Whisk the remaining ingredients with the finely chopped fennel tops. Season.
6 About 30 minutes before serving the salad, gently toss the vegetables in the dressing and allow to come to room temperature.

NOT SUITABLE FOR FREEZING
170 Calories per serving

COOK'S TIP
To prepare ahead, complete to the end of step 5 up to 1 day in advance. Finish as above.

MIXED LEAF, ORANGE AND STRAWBERRY SALAD

Preparation time: 20 minutes
Cooking time: nil

SERVES 6

1 small frisée lettuce
1 bunch of watercress
3 large oranges, peeled and sliced
225 g (8 oz) strawberries, sliced
1 large ripe avocado, peeled and sliced
45 ml (3 tbsp) olive oil
5 ml (1 tsp) white wine vinegar
5 ml (1 tsp) Dijon mustard
salt and pepper

1 Tear the frisée and watercress into small pieces and place in a large serving bowl.
2 Add the oranges, strawberries and avocado to the bowl.
3 Whisk together the olive oil, wine vinegar and Dijon mustard. Add seasoning to taste. Pour the dressing over the prepared salad. Toss well and serve.

NOT SUITABLE FOR FREEZING
150 Calories per serving

ARTICHOKE AND ASPARAGUS SALAD

Preparation time: 25 minutes plus marinating
Cooking time: 20–45 minutes

SERVES 6

6 small young or 3 large firm globe artichokes
350 g (12 oz) asparagus
125 ml (4 fl oz) olive oil
30 ml (2 tbsp) orange juice
30 ml (2 tbsp) chopped fresh herbs such as basil, lemon thyme and marjoram or 10 ml (2 tsp) dried herbs
salt and pepper
1 bunch of radishes
175 g (6 oz) mixed black and green olives, with stones
basil sprigs, to garnish (optional)
crusty bread, to serve

1 If using small artichokes, trim the stalk to within 4 cm (1½ inches) of the head and plunge into a saucepan of boiling salted water. Cover and simmer for 20–25 minutes or until the base is tender. Drain and plunge into cold water, then drain and pat dry on absorbent kitchen paper. Leave to cool.

2 If using large artichokes, break off the stalks. Snip off the sharp tips of the leaves. Cook in a large saucepan of boiling salted water for 35–45 minutes, weighing them down with a heatproof plate to keep them submerged. They are cooked when a central leaf can be pulled out easily. Drain and plunge into cold water, then drain and pat dry, as before. When completely cold, quarter each large artichoke and carefully scoop out the hairy choke at the base.

3 Trim any tough stalks from the asparagus, cut into 5 cm (2 inch) lengths and plunge into boiling salted water for 8–10 minutes or until tender but still crisp. Plunge into cold water and drain.

4 In a large bowl, whisk together the olive oil, orange juice, chopped herbs and salt and pepper

to taste. Add the cooked vegetables and toss well to coat.

5 Trim the radishes and halve or quarter, if necessary. Place the olives in a polythene bag and lightly 'crack' with a rolling pin. Add the radishes and olives to the vegetables and toss lightly. Cover and refrigerate for 4 hours or overnight. (The flavour is better the longer you leave it.)

6 Remove from the refrigerator 2 hours before serving. Serve with crusty bread and garnish with basil sprigs, if wished.

NOT SUITABLE FOR FREEZING
200 Calories per serving

ROASTED GREEK SALAD

Preparation time: 10 minutes plus marinating
Cooking time: 45 minutes

SERVES 4

225 g (8 oz) feta cheese
30 ml (2 tbsp) olive oil
2.5 ml (½ tsp) balsamic or red wine vinegar
15 ml (1 tbsp) lemon juice
30 ml (2 tbsp) chopped fresh thyme
black pepper
900 g (2 lb) courgettes, thickly sliced
4 garlic cloves, skinned and thinly sliced
225 g (8 oz) small red onions, skinned and thinly sliced
700 g (1½ lb) tomatoes, halved or quartered
50 g (2 oz) pitted black olives

1 Cut the feta cheese into 1 cm (½ inch) thick slices. Mix together 15 ml (1 tbsp) olive oil, the balsamic vinegar, lemon juice and half the chopped thyme. Season with plenty of black pepper. Pour over the feta and leave to marinate for at least 1 hour.

2 Place the courgettes, garlic and onions in a roasting tin with the remaining olive oil. Cook the vegetables at 230°C (450°F) mark 8 for 30 minutes, turning occasionally. Add the tomatoes, olives and remaining thyme. Cook for 10 minutes or until the vegetables are tender. Season.

3 Just before the end of the cooking time, drain the cheese from the marinade and place on a baking sheet. Cook in the oven for 5–7 minutes or until bubbling and slightly browned.

4 Serve the roasted vegetables with the remaining marinade and topped with feta cheese.

NOT SUITABLE FOR FREEZING
290 Calories per serving

COOK'S TIP
Use a fish slice to move the feta so that it doesn't break up. Season with black pepper only as feta cheese is very salty.

For a tasty alternative, substitute roughly chopped aubergine for half of the courgettes. Add at step 2 with the courgettes.

POTATO SALAD WITH YOGURT AND MUSTARD DRESSING

Preparation time: 10 minutes
Cooking time: 15 minutes

SERVES 4

This dressing can be made using either fromage frais or plain yogurt. If you use yogurt, try one of the 'bio' varieties, which have a milder, less acidic taste and will make a good creamy dressing. You can adjust the level of mustard to suit your own taste, and if you prefer something a little spicier, the same basic dressing tastes delicious mixed with a mild curry paste.

550 g (1 lb 4 oz) new potatoes, scrubbed
45 ml (3 tbsp) reduced-calorie mayonnaise
45 ml (3 tbsp) low-fat fromage frais or plain yogurt
2.5 ml (½ tsp) Dijon mustard
5 ml (1 tsp) wholegrain mustard
60 ml (4 tbsp) semi-skimmed milk
50 g (2 oz) fresh young spinach or watercress, roughly chopped
salt and pepper
flat-leaf parsley, to garnish

1 Cook the potatoes in boiling salted water for 15–20 minutes or until they are just tender. Drain and cool.

2 Whisk together the mayonnaise, fromage frais or yogurt, mustards and milk. Add the chopped spinach or watercress and seasoning.

3 Halve any large potatoes, then toss with the dressing and serve garnished with flat-leaf parsley.

NOT SUITABLE FOR FREEZING
170 Calories per serving

SPINACH, BACON AND OMELETTE SALAD

Preparation time: 5 minutes
Cooking time: 8 minutes

SERVES 2

Try to find small young spinach leaves as they're more tender than the older ones.

125 g (4 oz) ready-prepared spinach
4 rashers lean back bacon
5 ml (1 tsp) olive oil
2 eggs, beaten
salt and pepper
4 canned anchovies, drained
60 ml (4 tbsp) fat-free vinaigrette dressing
fresh chervil, to garnish

1 Tear the spinach into small pieces and place in a bowl.
2 Grill the bacon until quite crisp, drain on absorbent kitchen paper then snip into small pieces. Sprinkle over the spinach.
3 Heat the oil in a small non-stick frying pan. Season the eggs with plenty of freshly ground black pepper, add to the pan and fry until quite firm. Drain on absorbent kitchen paper. Cut into strips and mix into the spinach.
4 Mash or shred the anchovy fillets and mix with the dressing. Toss into the salad. Serve immediately, garnished with fresh chervil.

NOT SUITABLE FOR FREEZING
215 Calories per serving

WARM VEGETABLE SALAD

Preparation time: 10 minutes
Cooking time: 3 minutes

SERVES 2

You can use whatever vegetables you have available for this recipe. If you can't find bobby beans, use French beans instead.

50 g (2 oz) carrots, cut into thin batons
2 courgettes, sliced
50 g (2 oz) bobby beans, topped and tailed and cut into 2.5 cm (1 inch) lengths
50 g (2 oz) mangetouts, topped and tailed
50 g (2 oz) broccoli florets
7.5 ml (1½ tsp) Dijon mustard
15 ml (1 tbsp) lemon juice
45 ml (3 tbsp) low-calorie mayonnaise
salt and pepper
125 g (4 oz) cold cooked chicken, skin removed
chive flowers, to garnish

1 Cook all the vegetables in boiling salted water for 3 minutes. Drain.
2 Stir the Dijon mustard and lemon juice into the mayonnaise, season well, then mix with the vegetables. Spoon onto individual serving plates. Place strips of cold chicken on top of the vegetables and serve immediately, garnished with chive flowers.

NOT SUITABLE FOR FREEZING
180 Calories per serving

WINTER SALAD

Preparation time: 10 minutes
Cooking time: nil

SERVES 4

grated rind of ½ lemon
45 ml (3 tbsp) lemon juice
30 ml (2 tbsp) olive oil
150 ml (¼ pint) natural yogurt
salt and pepper
2 eating apples, cored and chopped
225 g (8 oz) red cabbage, shredded
1 small onion, skinned and finely sliced
4 celery sticks, finely sliced
125 g (4 oz) reduced-fat Cheddar cheese, cut into cubes
50 g (2 oz) unsalted peanuts in skins
celery leaves, to garnish

1 In a large bowl, whisk together the lemon rind and juice, olive oil and yogurt. Season well.
2 Toss the apples in the dressing.
3 Toss the cabbage, onion, celery and cheese with the apples, mixing well. Sprinkle with peanuts, garnish with celery leaves and serve.

NOT SUITABLE FOR FREEZING
290 Calories per serving

GRILLED CHICORY AND ASPARAGUS SALAD

Preparation time: 3 minutes
Cooking time: 5 minutes

SERVES 1

1 small head of chicory
75 g (3 oz) thin asparagus, trimmed
salt and pepper
25 g (1 oz) fresh Parmesan cheese, grated
fresh thyme, to garnish

1 Break up the chicory and place on a flameproof serving dish.
2 Cook the trimmed asparagus in boiling salted water for 2–3 minutes or until just tender. Drain and place on top of the chicory.
3 Sprinkle over the grated Parmesan and place under a medium grill for 2–3 minutes until the cheese starts to melt. Garnish with fresh thyme and serve.

NOT SUITABLE FOR FREEZING
175 Calories per serving

SEASONAL SALAD WITH BLUE CHEESE

Preparation time: 15 minutes
Cooking time: 20 minutes

SERVES 4

This dressing also makes a delicious filling for jacket potatoes and is wonderful served with a crisp green side salad.

1.1 kg (2¼ lb) seasonal vegetables, eg patty pan squash, French beans, aubergine, courgettes
15 ml (1 tbsp) olive oil
75 ml (5 tbsp) low-fat fromage frais
30 ml (2 tbsp) skimmed milk
75 g (3 oz) blue cheese, such as Stilton, crumbled
salt and pepper

1 Halve the patty pan squash, top and tail the French beans. Cook in a saucepan of boiling, salted water for about 5 minutes until just tender. Drain well. Chop the aubergine and slice the courgettes. Toss lightly in the oil and place under a hot grill for 10–15 minutes, turning once, until golden brown and tender.
2 Whisk together the fromage frais and the milk. Stir in the blue cheese. Season (remembering blue cheese is quite salty). Toss the warm vegetables in the dressing and serve.

NOT SUITABLE FOR FREEZING
150 Calories per serving

ROASTED PEPPERS WITH ORIENTAL DRESSING

Preparation time: 10 minutes
Cooking time: 15 minutes

SERVES 4

This salad is also delicious served warm. Simply reheat the peppers under the grill for 3–4 minutes and warm the dressing for 2–3 minutes in a saucepan.

2 red peppers
1 yellow pepper
1 orange pepper
½ small hot red chilli, deseeded and finely chopped
½ small hot green chilli, deseeded and finely chopped
15 g (½ oz) fresh root ginger, peeled and finely chopped
1 small bunch of spring onions, trimmed and sliced
60 ml (4 tbsp) soy sauce
60 ml (4 tbsp) lemon juice
15 ml (1 tbsp) white wine vinegar
30 ml (2 tbsp) runny honey

1 Cut the peppers in half and place under a hot grill for about 10–15 minutes or until the skin becomes blackened and charred. Cover with a clean damp tea towel and leave to cool.
2 Whisk the chillies with all the remaining ingredients until thoroughly combined.
3 Remove the skin and seeds from the charred peppers. Cut into thick slices. Spoon the dressing over the peppers and serve.

NOT SUITABLE FOR FREEZING
70 Calories per serving

VEGETARIAN MAIN COURSES

VEGETABLES WITH COCONUT AND CORIANDER

Preparation time: 10 minutes
Cooking time: 30 minutes

SERVES 4

125 g (4 oz) creamed coconut, grated
15 ml (1 tbsp) olive oil
125 g (4 oz) onions, skinned and finely chopped
15 ml (1 tbsp) plain flour
350 g (12 oz) cauliflower florets
700 g (1½ lb) pumpkin or swede, cut into chunks
10 ml (2 tsp) poppy seeds
150 ml (¼ pint) vegetable stock
425 g (15 oz) can lima or haricot beans, drained
salt and pepper
60 ml (4 tbsp) chopped fresh coriander

1 Place the creamed coconut in a bowl and pour over 300 ml (½ pint) boiling water.
2 Heat the oil in a saucepan, add the onions and cook for 2–3 minutes. Stir in the flour, cauliflower, pumpkin or swede and poppy seeds.
3 Pour in the coconut mixture and stock. Bring to the boil, cover and simmer for about 25 minutes or until the vegetables are just tender.
4 Add the beans. Cook, stirring, over a moderate heat for 2–3 minutes. Adjust the seasoning and stir in the coriander. Serve immediately.

NOT SUITABLE FOR FREEZING
290 Calories per serving

MUSHROOM AND SPINACH RISOTTO

Preparation time: 15 minutes
Cooking time: 30 minutes

SERVES 4

15 ml (1 tbsp) olive oil
175 g (6 oz) onion, skinned and chopped
175 g (6 oz) arborio (risotto) rice
grated rind of 1 lemon
750 ml (1¼ pints) hot vegetable stock
350 g (12 oz) mixed mushrooms, such as flat, brown cap and shiitake, quartered
225 g (8 oz) fresh spinach, shredded
15 ml (1 tbsp) lemon juice
salt and pepper
pinch of grated nutmeg

1 Heat the oil in a large saucepan, then add the chopped onion, cover and cook over a low heat for 5 minutes.
2 Stir in the rice, lemon rind and about one-third of the stock. Cook, stirring, for about 5 minutes.
3 Add half the remaining stock and cook, stirring, until it has been absorbed.
4 Add the remaining stock and cook, stirring, until almost all of it has been absorbed. Stir in the mushrooms, spinach and lemon juice and cook for 2–3 minutes, stirring occasionally. Adjust the seasoning, add a little grated nutmeg and serve at once.

NOT SUITABLE FOR FREEZING
332 Calories per serving

COOK'S TIP
Sprinkle with freshly grated Parmesan cheese to serve, if you like, but remember that this adds about 70 calories per 15 ml (1 tbsp).

WINTER VEGETABLES WITH LENTILS AND GINGER

Preparation time: 15 minutes
Cooking time: 16 minutes

SERVES 4

45 ml (3 tbsp) olive oil
5 ml (1 tsp) ground cumim
15 ml (1 tbsp) ground coriander
15 ml (1 tbsp) mustard powder
1 garlic clove, skinned and crushed
1 cm (½ inch) piece of fresh root ginger, peeled and chopped
225 g (8 oz) frozen baby onions
225 g (8 oz) button mushrooms, wiped and halved if necessary
225 g (8 oz) carrots, peeled and thinly sliced
225 g (8 oz) trimmed leeks, thickly sliced
275 g (10 oz) parsnips, peeled and diced
175 g (6 oz) split red lentils
900 ml (1½ pints) vegetable stock
30 ml (2 tbsp) chopped fresh coriander
salt and pepper
brown rice and poppadoms, to serve

1 Heat the oil in a large saucepan. Add the cumin, coriander, mustard, garlic and ginger and cook, stirring, for 1 minute.
2 Add all the remaining ingredients except the coriander and seasoning, bring to the boil, cover and simmer for 15 minutes or until the lentils are just tender. Stir in the coriander, adjust the seasoning and serve with brown rice and poppadoms.

NOT SUITABLE FOR FREEZING
290 Calories per serving

VEGETABLE COUSCOUS

Preparation time: 10 minutes
Cooking time: 15 minutes

SERVES 4

225 g (8 oz) quick-cook couscous
15 ml (1 tbsp) olive oil
2 garlic cloves, skinned and crushed
10 ml (2 tsp) ground cumin
2.5 ml (½ tsp) mild chilli powder
2.5 ml (½ tsp) ground ginger
60 ml (4 tbsp) tomato purée
1 bay leaf
1 vegetable stock cube
225 g (8 oz) aubergine, cut into chunks
175 g (6 oz) courgettes, cut into chunks
175 g (6 oz) carrots, peeled and cut into chunks
175 g (6 oz) onions, skinned and cut into chunks
175 g (6 oz) frozen broad beans, thawed, or canned chick peas, drained
salt and pepper
mild chilli powder and fresh herbs, to garnish

1 Put the couscous on a tray and soak according to the manufacturer's instructions.
2 Heat the oil in a saucepan (over which a metal sieve or colander will fit). Add the garlic and the spices and cook gently for 1 minute, stirring occasionally. Stir in the tomato purée, bay leaf and crumble in the vegetable stock cube.
3 Add the vegetables and broad beans or chick peas to the pan with the seasoning. Add 750 ml (1¼ pints) water, cover and boil for 8 minutes.
4 Meanwhile, fork the couscous to break up any lumps and spread in a metal sieve or colander lined with muslin or a clean J-cloth. Place over the vegetables, cover tightly and cook for 5 minutes or until the vegetables are tender, the sauce well reduced and the couscous piping hot. Adjust the seasoning of the vegetables.
5 Spoon the couscous onto a serving dish and pile the vegetables on top. Spoon over the cooking juices. Garnish with chilli powder and fresh herbs and serve.

NOT SUITABLE FOR FREEZING
260 Calories per serving

MUSHROOM RAGOUT

Preparation time: 15 minutes plus soaking
Cooking time: 35 minutes

SERVES 2

20 g (¾ oz) dried mushrooms
300 ml (½ pint) vegetable stock
225 g (8 oz) brown cap mushrooms, wiped and sliced
bunch of spring onions, trimmed and sliced
25 g (1 oz) butter
salt and pepper
45 ml (3 tbsp) crème fraîche
30 ml (2 tbsp) chopped fresh coriander
creme fraiche and fresh coriander, to garnish
pasta, to serve

1 Cover the dried mushrooms with the stock and leave to soak for 30 minutes. Drain, reserving the stock, and dry on absorbent kitchen paper.
2 Heat the butter in a heavy-based saucepan. Add all the mushrooms and half the spring onions and sauté for 10 minutes until tender.
3 Add the stock, bring to the boil and simmer for 15 minutes or until most of the liquid has been absorbed.
4 Add the remaining spring onions and season to taste. Stir in the crème fraîche and coriander and heat gently to warm through. Garnish with coriander and crème fraîche and serve with pasta.

NOT SUITABLE FOR FREEZING
235 Calories per serving

CARAMELIZED ONION AND GRUYÈRE FRITTATA

Preparation time: 10 minutes
Cooking time: 40 minutes

SERVES 4

30 ml (2 tbsp) olive oil
700 g (1½ lb) onions, skinned and sliced
1 garlic clove, skinned and crushed
4 eggs
15 ml (1 tbsp) each chopped fresh chives and parsley
salt and pepper
125 g (4 oz) fresh spinach, chopped
75 g (3 oz) each Gruyère and Edam cheese, diced

1 Heat the oil in a small, non-stick frying pan (about 19 cm (7½ inch) is ideal). Cook the onions and the garlic over a very gentle heat, covered, for 25–30 minutes or until caramelized and golden brown, stirring occasionally.

2 Beat together the eggs, herbs and plenty of seasoning. Remove the onions from the pan with a slotted spoon and add the spinach. Cook over a low heat, stirring, until wilted and all the excess moisture has evaporated. Return the onions to the pan with the cheese and stir until the mixture is thoroughly combined.

3 Pour in the egg mixture and allow it to run through the onions. Cook over a medium heat, loosening the edge of the frittata with a spatula as it sets, for about 3–4 minutes or until the base and the edge of the mixture are set. Cover the pan handle with foil and place under a hot grill for 3–4 minutes or until the top is set and golden brown and the cheese is bubbling. Serve.

NOT SUITABLE FOR FREEZING
330 Calories per serving

SUMMER COUSCOUS

Preparation time: 30 minutes
Cooking time: nil

SERVES 6

225 g (8 oz) couscous
6 spring onions, trimmed and chopped
3 tomatoes, diced
6 sun-dried tomatoes in oil, drained and diced
125 g (4 oz) black olives, pitted
30 ml (2 tbsp) chopped fresh mint
15 ml (1 tbsp) each chopped fresh coriander and parsley
2–3 garlic cloves, skinned and crushed
45 ml (3 tbsp) olive oil
juice of 1 lemon
salt and black pepper

1 Put the couscous in a large bowl and pour in 600 ml (1 pint) cold water. Leave to soak for 15–20 minutes or until all the liquid has been absorbed.

2 Stir all the remaining ingredients into the couscous and season well. Serve.

NOT SUITABLE FOR FREEZING
230 Calories per serving

SUMMER COUSCOUS

MUSHROOM RISOTTO CAKES

Preparation time: 10 minutes
Cooking time: 45 minutes

SERVES 4

15 g (½ oz) butter
1 garlic clove, skinned and crushed
125 g (4 oz) arborio (risotto) rice
175 g (6 oz) brown cap mushrooms, wiped and finely chopped
350 ml (12 fl oz) light stock
salt and pepper
75 g (3 oz) grated Parmesan cheese
30 ml (2 tbsp) chopped fresh parsley
40 g (1½ oz) wholemeal breadcrumbs
1 egg, beaten
fresh flat-leaf parsley, to garnish

1 Melt the butter in a large, non-stick saucepan. Stir in the garlic and the rice and cook, stirring, for 1–2 minutes. Add the mushrooms, stock and seasoning and bring to the boil.
2 Reduce the heat and cook, stirring occasionally, for 20 minutes or until all the liquid has been absorbed and the rice is tender. Remove from the heat and add 50 g (2 oz) Parmesan cheese and the parsley. Mix well.
3 Allow the mixture to cool. With wet hands, shape the mixture into 8 small, round cakes. Mix the breadcrumbs with the remaining Parmesan. Dip the cakes in the beaten egg then coat in the breacrumb mixture.
4 Place on a lightly greased baking sheet and cook at 190°C (375°F) mark 5 for 15–20 minutes or until warmed through. Garnish with flat-leaf parsley and serve.

NOT SUITABLE FOR FREEZING
295 Calories per serving

GOLDEN SPINACH BAKE

Preparation time: 15 minutes
Cooking time: 45 minutes

SERVES 4

175 g (6 oz) sliced white bread
350 ml (12 fl oz) skimmed milk
3 eggs
5 ml (1 tsp) Dijon mustard
salt and pepper
450 g (1 lb) frozen leaf spinach, thawed
150 ml (¼ pint) very low-fat fromage frais
2.5 ml (½ tsp) grated nutmeg
150 g (5 oz) reduced-fat Cheddar cheese, grated
shavings of reduced-fat Cheddar cheese and flat-leaf parsley, to garnish

1 Halve the bread slices and place in a shallow dish. Whisk together the milk, eggs, mustard and seasoning. Pour over the bread and leave to soak for 5 minutes or until most of the milk has been absorbed.
2 Drain the spinach well and chop. Mix with the fromage frais and nutmeg.
3 Place a layer of bread in a 1.1 litre (2 pint) ovenproof dish, followed by half the spinach and a third of the cheese. Repeat the layers until all the ingredients are used, ending with a layer of bread topped with cheese. Pour over any remaining milk and egg mixture.
4 Bake at 180°C (350°F) mark 4 for about 45 minutes or until lightly set and golden. Serve immediately, sprinkled with cheese and garnished with flat-leaf parsley.

NOT SUITABLE FOR FREEZING
240 Calories per serving

SPICED RATATOUILLE

Preparation time: 20 minutes
Cooking time: 40 minutes

SERVES 4

450 g (1 lb) aubergines, cut into chunks
salt and pepper
15 ml (1 tbsp) olive oil
350 g (12 oz) onions, skinned and chopped
2 red peppers, deseeded and chopped
2.5 ml (½ tsp) chilli powder
2 garlic cloves, skinned and crushed
450 g (1 lb) courgettes, sliced
two 400 g (14 oz) cans chopped tomatoes
5 ml (1 tsp) dried oregano
2 bay leaves
30 ml (2 tbsp) tomato purée

1 Sprinkle the aubergines with salt and leave to stand for about 20 minutes. Rinse under a cold tap to remove the salt and drain on absorbent kitchen paper.
2 Heat the oil in a large flameproof casserole. Add the aubergines, onions, peppers and chilli powder and cook, stirring, over a high heat for 2–3 minutes, or until the vegetables begin to soften.
3 Add the garlic and all the remaining ingredients. Bring to the boil, cover and simmer for 30–40 minutes, or until all the vegetables are soft and the liquid is reduced and thickened. Adjust the seasoning before serving.

SUITABLE FOR FREEZING
115 Calories per serving

TOMATO RISOTTO

Preparation time: 10 minutes
Cooking time: 15 minutes

SERVES 6

30 ml (2 tbsp) olive oil
125 g (4 oz) onion, skinned and finely chopped
350 g (12 oz) arborio (risotto) rice
pinch of saffron strands (optional)
275 g (10 oz) yellow cherry tomatoes, halved
1 large sprig of fresh rosemary
salt and pepper
60 ml (4 tbsp) dry white wine
750 ml (1¼ pints) hot vegetable stock

1 Heat the oil in a flameproof casserole and cook the onion for about 2–3 minutes or until beginning to soften. Stir in the rice and saffron, if using. Season well and pour in the wine and stock, stirring well to mix.
2 Bring to the boil, stirring, then cover and simmer for 5 minutes. Stir in the tomatoes and rosemary. Cover and simmer for 5–7 minutes or until the rice is tender and most of the liquid has been absorbed. Season and serve.

NOT SUITABLE FOR FREEZING
275 Calories per serving

VEGETABLES WITH A FETA CHEESE CRUST

Preparation time: 20 minutes
Cooking time: 1 hour 5 minutes

SERVES 6

2 large aubergines, about 675 g (1½ lb) total weight, trimmed and roughly chopped
450 g (1 lb) tomatoes, chopped
2 onions, skinned and chopped
4 celery sticks, trimmed and roughly chopped
2 bay leaves
5 ml (1 tsp) dried marjoram
45 ml (3 tbsp) tomato purée
150 ml (¼ pint) vegetable stock
400 g (14 oz) can artichoke hearts, drained and quartered
115 g (4 oz) pitted black olives
salt and pepper
50 g (2 oz) margarine
50 g (2 oz) plain flour
600 ml (1 pint) semi-skimmed milk
100 g (4 oz) feta cheese, crumbled
2 eggs, separated

1 Put the aubergines, tomatoes, onions, celery, bay leaves, marjoram, tomato purée and stock in a large shallow flameproof casserole. Bring to the boil and simmer for 15 minutes or until the vegetables are softened. Add the artichoke hearts, olives and seasoning.
2 Meanwhile, melt the margarine in a saucepan, stir in the flour and cook, stirring, for 1–2 minutes. Remove from the heat and stir in the milk. Bring to the boil, stirring, and simmer for 2–3 minutes. Remove from the heat and stir in the cheese and egg yolks. Whisk the egg whites until stiff then gently fold in to the cheese sauce, using a metal spoon. Season with pepper.
3 Spoon the cheese sauce over the vegetables to cover completely. Bake at 180°C (350°F)

mark 4 for about 50 minutes until golden brown. Serve hot.

NOT SUITABLE FOR FREEZING
274 Calories per serving

HOT SPICED CHICK PEA SALAD

Preparation time: 5 minutes
Cooking time: 10 minutes

SERVES 4

15 ml (1 tbsp) olive oil
125 g (4 oz) onion, skinned and chopped
10 ml (2 tsp) ground turmeric
15 ml (1 tbsp) cumin seeds
450 g (1 lb) tomatoes, chopped
two 400 g (14 oz) cans chick peas, drained
15 ml (1 tbsp) lemon juice
60 ml (4 tbsp) chopped fresh coriander
salt and pepper
coriander leaves, to garnish

1 Heat the oil in a saucepan and cook the onion until golden brown.
2 Add the turmeric and cumin seeds and cook, stirring, for 1–2 minutes. Add the remaining ingredients and heat through. Garnish with fresh coriander and serve.

NOT SUITABLE FOR FREEZING
345 Calories per serving

VEGETABLES WITH A FETA CHEESE CRUST

PASTA AND NOODLES

MIXED MUSHROOM PASTA

Preparation time: 20 minutes
Cooking time: 15 minutes

SERVES 4

You'll find dried mushrooms in delicatessens and supermarkets. You only need a very small amount to add a rich flavour to casseroles and soups.

15 g (½ oz) dried porcini mushrooms
225 g (8 oz) spaghetti
30 ml (2 tbsp) olive oil
1 small onion, skinned and finely chopped
1 garlic clove, skinned and crushed
225 g (8 oz) button or brown cap mushrooms, wiped and chopped
50 ml (2 fl oz) fromage frais
salt and pepper
fresh rosemary sprigs, to garnish

1 Soak the porcini mushrooms in 300 ml (½ pint) warm water for about 20 minutes. Drain, reserving the soaking liquid, and chop.

2 Cook the pasta in boiling, salted water until just tender.

3 Meanwhile, heat the oil in a saucepan and sauté the onion and garlic until just beginning to soften. Add all the mushrooms and sauté for 2–3 minutes. Add the reserved soaking liquid and boil for about 5 minutes or until reduced by half. Remove from the heat, stir in the fromage frais and season to taste.

4 Drain the pasta well and stir into the mushroom sauce. Garnish with fresh rosemary sprigs and serve immediately.

NOT SUITABLE FOR FREEZING
305 Calories per serving

PASTA WITH LEEKS AND LEMON MAYONNAISE

Preparation time: 15 minutes
Cooking time: 10 minutes

SERVES 4

60 ml (4 tbsp) reduced-calorie mayonnaise
150 ml (¼ pint) very low-fat fromage frais
grated rind of 1 lemon
15 ml (1 tbsp) lemon juice
1 garlic clove, skinned and crushed
salt and pepper
175 g (6 oz) dried pasta shapes
15 ml (1 tbsp) olive oil
700 g (1½ lb) trimmed leeks, sliced
225 g (8 oz) brown cap mushrooms, wiped and sliced
chopped fresh chives and finely grated lemon rind, to garnish

1 Mix together the mayonnaise, fromage frais, lemon rind and juice, crushed garlic and plenty of seasoning. Set aside.
2 Cook the pasta in boiling, salted water until just tender.
3 Meanwhile, heat the oil in a non-stick frying pan and sauté the leeks and mushrooms for 5–10 minutes or until golden brown and just softened. Season well.
4 Drain the pasta. Spoon the sautéed leeks and mushrooms over the hot pasta. Serve immediately with the lemon mayonnaise, garnished with the chives and lemon rind.

NOT SUITABLE FOR FREEZING
315 Calories per serving

SUN-DRIED TOMATO PASTA

Preparation time: 5 minutes
Cooking time: 25 minutes

SERVES 4

Sun-dried tomatoes add such a rich flavour to the sauce, you won't believe it's so low in calories. Double the quantity of sauce and keep some in the freezer, if you like.

15 ml (1 tbsp) olive oil
75 g (3 oz) onion, skinned and chopped
75 g (3 oz) carrot, peeled and chopped
75 g (3 oz) celery, chopped
1 garlic clove, skinned and crushed
two 400 g (14 oz) cans chopped tomatoes
125 g (4 oz) sun-dried tomatoes in olive oil, drained and chopped
150 ml (¼ pint) light stock
100 ml (4 fl oz) dry white wine
salt and pepper
225 g (8 oz) broad pasta, eg pappardelle, or spaghetti
shavings of pecorino or Parmesan cheese, to serve

1 Heat the oil in a large saucepan. Add the onion, carrot, celery and garlic and cook, stirring, for about 5 minutes, or until they start to soften.
2 Stir in the canned tomatoes, sun-dried tomatoes, stock, wine and seasoning. Simmer, covered, for 20 minutes, stirring occasionally.
3 Purée half the sauce in a food processor or blender. Return to the pan and stir into the remaining sauce.
4 Meanwhile, cook the pasta in boiling, salted water until just tender. Drain. Pour the sauce over the pasta, top with shavings of pecorino or Parmesan and serve.

SAUCE SUITABLE FOR FREEZING
300 Calories per serving

CRUNCHY VEGETABLE PASTA

Preparation time: 15 minutes
Cooking time: 15 minutes

SERVES 4

175 g (6 oz) dried pasta shapes
15 ml (1 tbsp) olive oil
125 g (4 oz) onion, skinned and finely chopped
1 garlic clove, skinned and crushed
1.25 ml (¼ tsp) mild chilli powder
1 red pepper, deseeded and diced
225 g (8 oz) tomatoes, diced
225 g (8 oz) courgettes, diced
350 ml (12 fl oz) tomato juice
15 ml (1 tbsp) red wine vinegar
salt and pepper
30 ml (2 tbsp) chopped fresh parsley
30 ml (2 tbsp) freshly grated Parmesan cheese

1 Cook the pasta in boiling, salted water until just tender.

2 Meanwhile, heat the oil in a non-stick frying pan and cook the onion and garlic for about 3 minutes or until beginning to soften. Add the chilli powder and cook, stirring, for a further minute.

3 Add the pepper, tomatoes and courgettes to the frying pan and cook over a medium heat for about 5 minutes or until heated through but still crisp. Stir in the tomato juice and vinegar and plenty of seasoning. Bring to the boil and simmer for 2–3 minutes or until piping hot.

4 Drain the pasta. Spoon the sauce over the pasta and serve immediately, sprinkled with the chopped parsley and Parmesan cheese.

SAUCE SUITABLE FOR FREEZING
260 Calories per serving

CAPPELLETTI WITH MUSHROOM SAUCE

Preparation time: 20 minutes
Cooking time: 15 minutes

SERVES 4

25 g (1 oz) dried porcini mushrooms
225 g (8 oz) cappelletti or other dried pasta shapes
25 g (1 oz) low-fat spread
1 onion, skinned and finely chopped
1 clove garlic, skinned and crushed
225 g (8 oz) button mushrooms, wiped and sliced
salt and pepper
15 ml (1 tbsp) chopped fresh chives
50 ml (2 fl oz) fromage frais

1 Soak the dried mushrooms in just enough warm water to cover, about 300 ml (½ pint), for about 20 minutes. Drain, reserving the soaking liquid, and slice.

2 Cook the pasta in boiling, salted water until just tender.

3 Meanwhile, melt the low-fat spread in a saucepan and cook the onion and garlic until softened. Add all the mushrooms and cook for 3–4 minutes. Add the soaking liquid and boil over a high heat for about 4–5 minutes, or until reduced by half. Season to taste.

4 Drain the pasta and stir into the mushroom sauce with the chives. Top with the fromage frais and serve.

NOT SUITABLE FOR FREEZING
265 Calories per serving

CRUNCHY VEGETABLE PASTA

SPINACH LASAGNE

Preparation time: 15 minutes
Cooking time: 1 hour

SERVES 4

800 g (1¾ lb) fresh spinach or 450 g (1 lb) frozen leaf spinach, thawed

15 ml (1 tbsp) chopped fresh marjoram or 5 ml (1 tsp) dried marjoram

salt and pepper

2.5 ml (½ tsp) grated nutmeg

350 g (12 oz) ricotta cheese or low-fat curd cheese

10 ml (2 tsp) olive oil, plus extra for greasing

225 g (8 oz) mushrooms, wiped and sliced

150 ml (¼ pint) vegetable stock

5 ml (1 tsp) soy sauce

8 or 9 strips of fresh lasagne

50 g (2 oz) Cheddar or Parmesan cheese, grated

1 If using fresh spinach, remove the stalks, wash the leaves and put in a large saucepan (without adding water) and cook gently for 5–7 minutes, stirring occasionally. Drain well and chop. If using frozen spinach, squeeze out all the water. Put the spinach into a bowl, add the marjoram and season with salt, pepper and nutmeg. Leave to cool. Stir in the ricotta cheese.

2 Heat the oil in a large saucepan and cook the mushrooms for about 10 minutes. Add the stock, bring to the boil and simmer for 5 minutes.

3 Purée the mushroom mixture in a food processor or blender, add the soy sauce and season. Place half of the spinach in the bottom of a 2.3 litre (4 pint) ovenproof dish, cover with two or three sheets of lasagne and one-third of the mushroom sauce. Add two or three more sheets of lasagne. Repeat the layers, ending with mushroom sauce. Sprinkle with cheese and bake at 200°C (400°F) mark 6 for 30–40 minutes.

NOT SUITABLE FOR FREEZING
330 Calories per serving

VEGETABLE, PASTA AND LENTIL POT

Preparation time: 25 minutes
Cooking time: 35 minutes

SERVES 4

450 g (1 lb) onion, carrot and celery, mixed

350 g (12 oz) mixed green vegetables, such as broccoli, courgettes and French beans

50 g (2 oz) smoked streaky bacon or chorizo

15 ml (1 tbsp) olive oil

2 garlic cloves, skinned and crushed

75 g (3 oz) green lentils

1.4 litres (2½ pints) ham or chicken stock

75 g (3 oz) tortelloni

salt and pepper

chopped fresh parsley, to garnish

1 Finely chop the onion, carrot and celery. Cut the remaining vegetables into bite-size pieces. Roughly chop the bacon or chorizo.

2 Heat the oil in a large saucepan and add the onion, carrot, celery, bacon and garlic. Cook over a moderate heat until beginning to brown.

3 Stir in the lentils and the stock. Bring to the boil, cover and simmer for 10 minutes.

4 Stir in the tortelloni, cover and simmer for a further 10 minutes. Add the remaining vegetables, cover and simmer for 5 minutes or until tender.

5 Adjust the seasoning, garnish with chopped fresh parsley and serve.

NOT SUITABLE FOR FREEZING
255 Calories per serving

SEAFOOD SPAGHETTI WITH PEPPER AND ALMOND SAUCE

Preparation time: 15 minutes
Cooking time: 20 minutes

SERVES 4

1 small red pepper, about 150 g (5 oz)
1 hot red chilli
50 g (2 oz) toasted blanched almonds
2–3 garlic cloves
30 ml (2 tbsp) red wine vinegar
350 ml (12 fl oz) tomato juice
60 ml (4 tbsp) chopped fresh parsley
salt and pepper
450 g (1 lb) mixed cooked seafood, eg prawns, mussels and squid
25 g (1 oz) spaghetti
chopped fresh chilli, to garnish

1 Place the pepper and chilli under the grill and cook, turning occasionally, until the skins have charred and blackened. Cover with a clean damp tea towel and leave to cool. Peel off the skins. Halve, discard the seeds, then put the flesh into a food processor or blender.
2 Add the almonds, garlic, vinegar, tomato juice, half the parsley and seasoning. Blend until almost smooth. Transfer to a saucepan.
3 Gently heat the sauce until simmering, then add the seafood. Simmer for 3–4 minutes until heated through, stirring frequently. Adjust the seasoning.
4 Meanwhile, cook the pasta in boiling, salted water until just tender. Drain, toss in the remaining parsley and season. Pour the sauce over the spaghetti, garnish with chopped fresh chilli and serve.

NOT SUITABLE FOR FREEZING
305 Calories per serving

PASTA SALAD WITH CHICKEN AND PESTO

Preparation time: 15 minutes
Cooking time: 10 minutes

SERVES 4

125 g (4 oz) mixed tomato, spinach and egg dried pasta shapes
salt and pepper
15 ml (1 tbsp) olive oil
30 ml (2 tbsp) red pesto
15 ml (1 tbsp) lemon juice
1 garlic clove, skinned and crushed
225 g (8 oz) roast chicken, skin removed
175 g (6 oz) cherry tomatoes, halved
6 spring onions, sliced
1 small fennel bulb, sliced
30 ml (2 tbsp) chopped fresh mixed herbs
15 ml (1 tbsp) toasted walnut pieces

1 Cook the pasta in boiling, salted water until just tender.
2 Meanwhile, in a large bowl, mix together the olive oil, pesto, lemon juice and garlic.
3 Drain the pasta and, while still warm, stir in the pesto mixture. Leave to cool.
4 Cut the chicken into strips and add to the cooled pasta with the tomatoes, spring onions and fennel. Season well.
5 Turn into a serving bowl, sprinkle with the herbs and toasted walnut pieces and serve.

NOT SUITABLE FOR FREEZING
330 Calories per serving

OVERLEAF

LEFT: SEAFOOD SPAGHETTI WITH PEPPER AND ALMOND SAUCE

RIGHT: PASTA WITH PAN-FRIED SALMON (PAGE 102)

PASTA WITH PAN-FRIED SALMON

Preparation time: 10 minutes
Cooking time: 20 minutes

SERVES 4

275 g (10 oz) salmon fillet, skinned
15 ml (1 tbsp) olive oil
15 ml (1 tbsp) plain flour
300 ml (½ pint) skimmed milk
30 ml (2 tbsp) chopped fresh parsley
30 ml (2 tbsp) capers
50 g (2 oz) can anchovy fillets, drained and finely chopped
1 garlic clove, skinned and crushed
5 ml (1 tsp) Dijon mustard
15 ml (1 tbsp) lemon juice
salt and pepper
125 g (4 oz) dried pasta shapes
flat-leaf parsley sprigs, to garnish

1 Cut the salmon into thick slices. Heat the oil in a non-stick frying pan and cook the salmon for 5–7 minutes, turning once.
2 Mix the flour to a paste with a little of the milk. Put in a saucepan with the remaining milk, 150 ml (¼ pint) water and the remaining ingredients. Bring slowly to the boil, stirring. Simmer for 2–3 minutes. Season (don't add too much salt as anchovies are salty).
3 Meanwhile, cook the pasta in boiling salted water until tender. Drain.
4 Arrange the salmon on a bed of pasta, spoon the sauce over, garnish with parsley and serve.

NOT SUITABLE FOR FREEZING
340 Calories per serving

COOK'S TIP
If you find anchovies too salty, soak them in milk for about 20 minutes. Drain before use.

CHILLI PORK WITH NOODLES

Preparation time: 15 minutes
Cooking time: 15 minutes

SERVES 4

The soy sauce should add sufficient salt to this dish, so simply season it with some freshly ground black pepper.

350 g (12 oz) pork fillet
225 g (8 oz) yellow pepper
225 g (8 oz) broccoli
30 ml (2 tbsp) olive oil
125 g (4 oz) onion, skinned and chopped
2.5 ml (½ tsp) mild chilli powder or a few drops of Tabasco sauce
5 ml (1 tsp) dried oregano or dried mixed herbs
50 g (2 oz) rice noodles or dried pasta
30 ml (2 tbsp) sherry or medium white wine
450 ml (1¼ pints) beef stock
15 ml (1 tbsp) hoisin or soy sauce
black pepper

1 Trim the pork of any excess fat and cut into thin slices. Deseed the pepper, then cut into similar-size pieces. Thinly slice the broccoli stalks and divide the remainder into small florets.
2 Heat the oil in a large non-stick sauté pan or wok and cook the pork for 2–3 minutes until browned. Remove with a slotted spoon and then drain on absorbent kitchen paper. Add all the vegetables, the chilli powder and herbs and cook, stirring, for 1–2 minutes.
3 Stir in the pork, the noodles, sherry or wine, stock and hoisin or soy sauce. Bring to the boil, cover and simmer for about 7 minutes or until all the ingredients are tender. Adjust the seasoning and serve.

NOT SUITABLE FOR FREEZING
285 Calories per serving

PASTA SALAD WITH AVOCADO DRESSING

Preparation time: 15 minutes
Cooking time: 10–12 minutes

SERVES 6

225 g (8 oz) pasta shapes
100 g (4 oz) asparagus, trimmed, tips removed and stalks cut into 2.5 cm (1 inch) pieces
2 courgettes, sliced
1 large ripe avocado
200 g (7 oz) very low-fat fromage frais
15 ml (1 tbsp) lemon juice
1 garlic clove, skinned and crushed
salt and pepper
1 eating apple, cored and chopped
30 ml (2 tbsp) chopped fresh coriander
15 g (½ oz) shelled pistachios, chopped

1 Cook the pasta in boiling, salted water, until tender.

2 Add the asparagus stalks 7 minutes before the end of cooking time. Add the courgettes and asparagus tips 2–3 minutes before the end of cooking time.

3 When the pasta is cooked, drain, rinse under cold running water then drain again. Place in a large bowl.

4 Cut the avocado in half, remove the stone then scoop out the flesh from one half and mash in a bowl. Add the fromage frais, lemon juice, garlic and salt and pepper and mix well together.

5 Chop the remaining avocado half into small pieces. Pour the avocado dressing over the pasta and add the chopped avocado and apple. Toss together until mixed, then sprinkle with the coriander and pistachios. Serve at once.

NOT SUITABLE FOR FREEZING
235 Calories per serving

PASTA WITH PESTO

Preparation time: 10 minutes
Cooking time: 15 minutes

SERVES 4

50 g (2 oz) garlic cloves, skinned
40 g (1½ oz) fresh basil
275 g (10 oz) very low-fat fromage frais
30 ml (2 tbsp) olive oil
salt and pepper
225 g (8 oz) dried pasta, such as tagliatelle
50 g (2 oz) fresh Parmesan cheese
fresh basil leaves, to garnish

1 Place the garlic cloves in a saucepan of boiling, salted water. Cover and simmer for 10 minutes or until soft. Drain well.

2 Pull the leaves off the basil stalks and put the leaves, garlic, fromage frais, olive oil and seasoning in a blender or food processor and process until smooth. Adjust the seasoning, if necessary.

3 Meanwhile, cook the pasta in boiling, salted water until tender. Drain and return to the pan. Add the sauce and stir over a moderate heat for 1–2 minutes.

4 Shave the Parmesan cheese over the top, garnish with fresh basil leaves and serve.

NOT SUITABLE FOR FREEZING
370 Calories per serving

GINGERED CHICKEN WITH NOODLES

Preparation time: 5 minutes
Cooking time: 15–20 minutes

SERVES 4

275 g (10 oz) skinless chicken breast fillet
15 ml (1 tbsp) olive oil
1 bunch of spring onions, trimmed and sliced
2.5 cm (1 inch) piece fresh root ginger, peeled and grated
1 garlic clove, skinned and crushed
30 ml (2 tbsp) mild curry paste or 15 ml (1 tbsp) Thai hot curry paste
300 ml (½ pint) coconut milk (see Cook's Tip)
about 300 ml (½ pint) chicken stock
salt and pepper
125 g (4 oz) Chinese egg noodles
10 ml (2 tsp) lemon or lime juice

1 Cut the chicken into bite-size pieces.
2 Heat the oil in a large, non-stick sauté pan and cook the spring onions, ginger and garlic until just beginning to soften. Add the chicken pieces and curry paste and cook for a further 5 minutes or until the chicken is golden.
3 Stir in the coconut milk, stock and seasoning and bring to the boil. Break the noodles in half and add to the pan. Cover and simmer for 5–10 minutes, stirring occasionally, until the noodles are just tender. Add a little more stock if the mixture becomes too dry. Add the lemon or lime juice, season to taste and serve immediately.

NOT SUITABLE FOR FREEZING
310 Calories per serving

COOK'S TIP
You can buy coconut milk in cans, or use 50 g (2 oz) creamed coconut, roughly chopped and dissolved in 300 ml (½ pint) boiling water.

PASTA NIÇOISE

Preparation time: 15 minutes, plus standing
Cooking time: 10–12 minutes

SERVES

225 g (8 oz) pasta shapes, such as shells, bows or twists
salt and pepper
225 g (8 oz) fresh or frozen fine green beans
225 g (8 oz) tomatoes, quartered
2 hard-boiled eggs, quartered
½ small cucumber, thinly sliced
50 g (2 oz) pitted black olives
15 ml (1 tbsp) capers
60 ml (4 tbsp) olive oil
7.5 ml (½ tbsp) lemon juice
pinch of sugar
2.5 ml (½ tsp) Dijon mustard
15 ml (1 tbsp) chopped fresh parsley
15 ml (1 tbsp) chopped fresh basil

1 Cook the pasta in boiling, salted water until tender. Top and tail the fresh beans, if using. Add the fresh or frozen beans to the pasta for the last 5 minutes of the cooking time, returning the water to the boil. Drain the pasta and beans, rinse under cold running water and drain again.
2 Put the pasta and beans in a salad bowl. Arrange the tomatoes, eggs, cucumber, olives and capers on top.
3 Put the oil, lemon juice, sugar, mustard, salt and pepper in a bowl and whisk together. Add the parsley and basil and mix well.
4 Pour the dressing over the salad, then allow to stand for 30 minutes before serving.

NOT SUITABLE FOR FREEZING
276 calories per serving

GINGERED CHICKEN WITH NOODLES

STIR-FRIED NOODLES WITH SHREDDED GREEN VEGETABLES

Preparation time: 15 minutes
Cooking time: 10 minutes

SERVES 4

175 g (6 oz) thread egg noodles
45 ml (3 tbsp) vegetable oil
4 spring onions, trimmed, quartered and shredded
1 courgette, quartered and shredded
½ green pepper, deseeded and cut into thin strips
75 g (3 oz) spinach, finely shredded
2.5 cm (1 inch) piece of fresh root ginger, peeled and chopped
1 garlic clove, skinned and crushed
1 chicken stock cube, crumbled
15 ml (1 tbsp) hoisin sauce
salt and pepper
celery leaves, to garnish

1 Bring a large saucepan of salted water to the boil, add the noodles, remove from the heat and leave to soak for 4 minutes. Drain well.

2 Heat 30 ml (2 tbsp) oil in a wok or large frying pan. Add the vegetables, ginger and garlic and stir-fry for 2 minutes.

3 Add the remaining oil to the pan, then add the noodles and stir-fry for 2 minutes. Add the crumbled stock cube, hoisin sauce and 15 ml (1 tbsp) water and cook for 2 minutes, lifting and mixing the noodles with two forks. Season with pepper, garnish and serve immediately.

NOT SUITABLE FOR FREEZING
300 Calories per serving

TAGLIATELLE WITH TOMATO SAUCE

Preparation time: 10 minutes
Cooking time: 40 minutes

SERVES 6

30 ml (2 tbsp) olive oil
1 small onion, skinned and finely chopped
2 celery sticks, trimmed and finely chopped
2 carrots, peeled and finely chopped
2 garlic cloves, skinned and crushed
two 400 g (14 oz) cans chopped tomatoes
30 ml (2 tbsp) tomato purée
150 ml (¼ pint) dry white wine
salt and pepper
450 g (1 lb) dried tagliatelle

1 Heat the oil in a large saucepan, add the onion, celery and carrots and cook, stirring, for 8–10 minutes until soft.

2 Stir in the garlic, tomatoes, tomato purée and wine. Season with salt and pepper, cover and simmer for 30 minutes, stirring occasionally.

3 Put about half the tomato sauce in a food processor or blender and purée until smooth. Stir into the remaining sauce and reheat gently.

4 Meanwhile, cook the tagliatelle in boiling, salted water for 8–10 minutes until just tender. Drain and transfer to a serving bowl. Pour over the sauce and serve immediately.

SAUCE SUITABLE FOR FREEZING
350 Calories per serving

SWEET THINGS

VANILLA POACHED PEARS

Preparation time: 15 minutes plus chilling
Cooking time: 20 minutes

SERVES 6

200 ml (7 fl oz) dry white wine

45 ml (3 tbsp) lemon juice

50 g (2 oz) caster sugar

1 vanilla pod, split, plus a few drops of vanilla essence

6 firm but ripe pears, about 800–900 g (1¾–2 lb) total weight

fresh bay leaves and Caramel Lattices (see below), to decorate (optional)

crème fraîche or soured cream, to serve

1 Put the wine, lemon juice, caster sugar, vanilla pod and a few drops of vanilla essence in a large saucepan with 450 ml (¾ pint) water. Stir gently over a low heat until all the sugar has dissolved.

2 Peel and halve the pears, but don't core them. Add to the wine mixture. Bring to the boil, then simmer, covered, for 12–15 minutes until the pears look slightly translucent but are still firm.

3 Using a slotted spoon, lift out the pears and place in a bowl. Boil the juices to reduce slightly. Add a little more vanilla essence if wished. Strain the syrup over the pears. Leave to cool, cover and refrigerate until needed.

4 Decorate, if wished, with fresh bay leaves and Caramel Lattices. Serve one pear half per person with a little syrup spooned over, with crème fraîche or soured cream. Place the remaining pears in a serving dish to offer as second helpings.

NOT SUITABLE FOR FREEZING
100 Calories per serving (per pear)

CARAMEL LATTICES

Preparation time: 15 minutes
Cooking time: 3–5 minutes

MAKES 6

It's important to work quickly when making these, or the caramel will set in the pan. The lattices are very brittle, so ease them off the spoons gently.

oil for greasing
75 g (3 oz) granulated sugar

1 Oil the back of six stainless steel table- or dessertspoons. Place them on a wire rack over an oiled baking sheet.
2 Place the sugar in a small, heavy-based saucepan with 45 ml (3 tbsp) water. Heat gently, stirring occasionally, until the sugar dissolves. Increase the heat and boil until the mixture turns a golden caramel colour.
3 Immediately take the pan off the heat and dip the base in and out of cold water, stirring all the time to prevent it setting.
4 While the caramel is still liquid but beginning to thicken, drizzle it from the end of a dessertspoon, moving it back and forth over the oiled spoons to create caramel lattices. Work quickly before the caramel sets.
5 Leave to harden then gently ease the lattices off the spoons. Store in an airtight containter for no more than 3 days.

NOT SUITABLE FOR FREEZING
50 Calories per lattice

RED FRUIT MALLOW

Preparation time: 10–20 minutes
Cooking time: 25–30 minutes

SERVES 6

450 g (1 lb) Bramley cooking apples or 350 g (12 oz) can or jar stewed apples with no added sugar
15 ml (1 tbsp) light soft brown sugar
225 g (8 oz) mixed berries, eg sliced strawberries, blackberries, and redcurrants (see Cook's Tip)
3 egg whites
175 g (6 oz) caster sugar
25 g (1 oz) skinned hazelnuts, chopped
thick Jersey cream, to serve

1 If using cooking apples, peel, core and roughly chop them, then place in a saucepan with the brown sugar and 15 ml (1 tbsp) water. Cook, stirring, over a gentle heat until the apples have become soft but not too pulpy. Leave to cool. If using ready-stewed apples, sweeten to taste but do not cook. Mix the berries with the apple and divide evenly among six 150 ml (¼ pint) ramekins or individual ovenproof dishes.
2 Whisk the egg whites until they just stand in peaks, then gradually whisk in the caster sugar, adding about 15 ml (1 tbsp) at a time until all the sugar has been incorporated and the mixture is thick and shiny.
3 Spoon the meringue mixture into a piping bag fitted with a 2.5 cm (1 inch) plain nozzle and pipe in circles on top of the fruit to form a pyramid, or spoon the meringue over the fruit in a tall mound. Sprinkle with the hazelnuts.
4 Bake at 180°C (350°F) mark 4 for 20–25 minutes or until lightly golden. Serve with thick Jersey cream.

NOT SUITABLE FOR FREEZING
195 Calories per serving

RED FRUIT MALLOW

BURNT CREAMS WITH SPICED FRUIT

Preparation time: 10 minutes
Cooking time: 15 minutes

SERVES 4

175 g (6 oz) dried apple rings
50 g (2 oz) no-soak pitted prunes
50 g (2 oz) no-soak dried apricots
pared rind and juice of 1 orange
pared rind of 1 lemon
15 ml (1 tbsp) lemon juice
pinch each of ground cloves and grated nutmeg
1 cinnamon stick
150 ml (¼ pint) low-fat natural yogurt
30 ml (2 tbsp) runny honey
10 ml (2 tsp) demerara sugar

1 Place the fruit in a saucepan with 600 ml (1 pint) water, the orange and lemon rind and juice, the ground cloves, grated nutmeg and the cinnamon stick. Bring to the boil and simmer gently for about 10 minutes until the fruit is tender but not too soft.
2 Meanwhile, mix together the yogurt and honey until smooth and blended.
3 Drain the fruit, reserving the juices, and arrange on four flameproof serving plates. Pour over a little of the juices. Spoon the yogurt on top and sprinkle with a little demerara sugar.
4 Grill until the topping is bubbling and golden brown. Serve immediately.

NOT SUITABLE FOR FREEZING
160 Calories per serving

HOT PINEAPPLE AND BANANA SALAD

Preparation time: 15 minutes
Cooking time: 12 minutes

SERVES 4

25 g (1 oz) low-fat spread
7.5 ml (1½ tsp) soft brown sugar
1 small pineapple, about 900 g (2 lb), peeled, cored and sliced
4 small bananas, about 450 g (1 lb) total weight, peeled and thickly sliced
30 ml (2 tbsp) Malibu, rum or orange juice
FOR THE COCONUT SAUCE (OPTIONAL)
50 g (2 oz) creamed coconut

1 Melt the low-fat spread in a large sauté pan, add 5 ml (1 tsp) sugar and cook for 1 minute. Add the pineapple and sauté gently for 3–4 minutes, until beginning to soften and brown. Add the bananas and sauté for 3 minutes. Pour in the Malibu, rum or orange juice and heat gently.
2 Meanwhile, make the coconut sauce. Place the creamed coconut and 75 ml (3 fl oz) boiling water in a small saucepan. Stir until the coconut dissolves. Add the remaining sugar. Gently bring to the boil and simmer for 1 minute. Serve with the warm fruit.

NOT SUITABLE FOR FREEZING
190 Calories per serving without the coconut sauce
230 Calories per serving with the coconut sauce

CHOCOLATE MUFFINS

Preparation time: 15 minutes
Cooking time: 20 minutes

SERVES 6

65 g (2½ oz) self-raising flour
1.25 ml (¼ tsp) baking powder
small pinch of salt
30 ml (2 tbsp) low-fat instant drinking chocolate powder
15 ml (1 tbsp) vegetable oil
2.5 ml (½ tsp) vanilla essence
1 egg, beaten
25 ml (5 tsp) skimmed milk
25 g (1 oz) plain chocolate, chopped
15 g (½ oz) walnuts, chopped

FOR THE CHOCOLATE SAUCE
45 ml (3 tbsp) low-fat instant drinking chocolate powder
10 ml (2 tsp) arrowroot

1 Sift the flour and baking powder into a bowl, add the salt and 30 ml (2 tbsp) drinking chocolate.
2 Make a well in the centre and add the oil, vanilla essence, egg and milk, then beat well until smooth. Gently stir in the chocolate and walnuts.
3 Place six individual paper muffin cases on a baking sheet. Spoon the mixture into the cases – it should be about 5 mm (¼ inch) from the top. Bake at 220°C (425°F) mark 7 for 15 minutes or until firm to the touch and well risen.
4 Meanwhile, make the chocolate sauce. Place the remaining drinking chocolate powder in a small saucepan with the arrowroot. Stir in 100 ml (4 fl oz) cold water to form a smooth paste. Add a further 175 ml (6 fl oz) cold water.
5 Slowly bring to the boil and then cook for 30 seconds, stirring all the time. Turn out the muffins and serve warm with the chocolate sauce.

NOT SUITABLE FOR FREEZING
160 Calories per serving

PEARS IN FILO

Preparation time: 25 minutes
Cooking time: 25 minutes

SERVES 4

75 g (3 oz) no-soak pitted prunes, finely chopped
25 g (1 oz) pecan nuts or walnuts, finely chopped
15 ml (1 tbsp) demerara sugar
pinch of ground cinnamon
30 ml (2 tbsp) unsweetened apple or orange juice
grated rind and juice of ½ lemon
4 ripe pears, preferably Williams, about 550 g (1¼ lb) total weight
4 sheets of filo pastry, each about 28 cm (11 inch) square
25 g (1 oz) low-fat spread, melted
fromage frais, to serve

1 Mix the prunes and nuts with the sugar, cinnamon, apple or orange juice and lemon rind and juice.
2 Peel the pears, cut off the stalks and remove the cores with an apple corer, leaving the pears whole.
3 Place each pear in the centre of a square of filo pastry, then fill the centre of the pear with the prune mixture. Wrap the pastry around each pear to enclose completely, pinching the top of the pastry to form a purse. Lightly brush with the melted low-fat spread.
4 Bake at 190°C (375°F) mark 5 for 20–25 minutes or until crisp, golden brown and cooked through, covering loosely with foil if necessary to prevent over-browning. Serve immediately, with fromage frais.

NOT SUITABLE FOR FREEZING
190 Calories per serving

OVERLEAF:
LEFT: CHOCOLATE BROWNIES (PAGE 114)
RIGHT: CHOCOLATE AND APRICOT ROULADE

CHOCOLATE BROWNIES

Preparation time: 15 minutes
Cooking time: 30 minutes

MAKES 15 SQUARES

175 g (6 oz) very low-fat spread
125 g (4 oz) dark soft brown sugar
150 g (5 oz) self-raising wholemeal flour
5 ml (1 tsp) baking powder
30 ml (2 tbsp) cocoa powder
50 g (2 oz) walnut pieces
50 g (2 oz) milk chocolate drops
3 eggs, lightly beaten
45 ml (3 tbsp) skimmed-milk
thin skimmed-milk custard and chocolate shavings, to serve

1 Lightly grease a 3.5 cm (1½ inch) deep, 27.5 x 17.5 cm (10 ¾ x 7 inch) cake tin then line with non-stick baking parchment.
2 Place the low-fat spread and sugar in a saucepan and heat gently until the sugar has dissolved. Leave to cool slightly.
3 Place the flour, baking powder and cocoa powder in a bowl. Stir in the nuts (roughly chopped if large) and the chocolate drops.
4 Make a well in the centre and then pour in the cooled sugar mixture and the eggs and milk. Beat well until thoroughly blended. Pour into the prepared cake tin.
5 Bake at 180°C (350°F) mark 4 for about 30–35 minutes or until just firm to the touch.
6 Allow to cool slightly in the tin, then turn out on to a wire rack and leave to cool completely. Cut into 15 squares and serve with thin skimmed-milk custard and shavings of chocolate.

SUITABLE FOR FREEZING
160 Calories per square

FROZEN STRAWBERRY ICE

Preparation time: 15 minutes plus freezing
Cooking time: nil

SERVES 4

450 g (1 lb) strawberries, hulled
150 ml (¼ pint) low-fat or low-calorie vanilla ice cream, slightly softened
150 ml (¼ pint) low-fat bio natural yogurt
15 ml (1 tbsp) framboise or cassis liqueur
2 egg whites
juice of 2 oranges
strawberry leaves, to decorate

1 In a food processor or blender, purée half the strawberries with the ice cream, yogurt and liqueur until smooth.
2 In a clean, dry bowl, whisk the egg whites until they just form soft peaks. Fold into the strawberry mixture. Divide among six individual ramekins and freeze for at least 4 hours, preferably overnight.
3 Slice the remaining strawberries and put into a bowl. Add the orange juice, cover and marinate for about 1 hour.
4 To serve, dip the outside of the ramekins into warm water for a few seconds and turn out onto serving plates. Leave at room temperature for about 10 minutes to soften a little before serving with the marinated strawberries, decorated with strawberry leaves.

SUITABLE FOR FREEZING
110 Calories per serving

CHOCOLATE AND APRICOT ROULADE

Preparation time: 30 minutes
Cooking time: 20 minutes

SERVES 8

50 g (2 oz) plain chocolate
30 ml (2 tbsp) cocoa powder
30 ml (2 tbsp) skimmed milk
3 eggs, separated
75 g (3 oz) caster sugar plus 10 ml (2 tsp)
two 400 g (14 oz) cans apricot halves in natural juice
10 ml (2 tsp) brandy (optional)
150 ml (¼ pint) low-fat natural fromage frais
icing sugar for dusting

1 Grease a 23 x 33 cm (9 x 13 inch) Swiss roll tin and line with baking parchment.
2 Break the chocolate into a bowl, put over a saucepan of simmering water and heat gently until melted. Remove from the heat and stir in the cocoa powder and milk.
3 Whisk the egg yolks and 75 g (3 oz) sugar until very thick and pale. Beat in the chocolate mixture. Whisk the egg whites until stiff, then fold into the chocolate mixture. Pour into the prepared tin and gently spread out.
4 Bake at 180°C (350°F) mark 4 for 20–25 minutes or until well risen and firm. Turn out on to a piece of baking parchment sprinkled with 10 ml (2 tsp) sugar. Carefully peel off the lining paper. Cover with a damp tea towel and leave to cool.
5 Drain the apricots and purée one can in a food processor until smooth. Chop the remaining apricots and fold into the purée with the brandy, if using. Spread the fromage frais over the roulade to within 1 cm (½ inch) of the edges, then top with the apricot mixture.
6 Starting from one of the narrow ends, carefully roll up the roulade, lifting the baking parchment to help it roll. Transfer the roulade to a serving plate, dust with icing sugar, slice and serve.

NOT SUITABLE FOR FREEZING
185 Calories per serving

COOK'S TIP
To prepare in advance, make the roulade and the apricot mixture the day before. Complete 2 hours before serving.

POACHED KUMQUATS

Preparation time: 5 minutes, plus chilling
Cooking time: 20 minutes

225 g (8 oz) kumquats
300 ml (½ pint) orange juice
45 ml (3 tbsp) sugar

1 Halve each kumquat, discarding any pips, and place in a saucepan with the orange juice and sugar. Bring slowly to the boil then simmer for about 15 minutes or until the kumquats are tender.
2 Remove the kumquats from the saucepan using a slotted spoon and set aside. Boil the orange juice until only about 90 ml (6 tbsp) remains. Pour over the kumquats and leave to cool. Cover and refrigerate until required.

SUITABLE FOR FREEZING
60 Calories per serving

FRESH FRUIT JELLY

Preparation time: 10 minutes plus chilling
Cooking time: 5 minutes

SERVES 6

If you don't have any small jelly moulds, use small tumblers or cups.

juice of 4 large lemons
30 ml (2 tbsp) powdered gelatine
900 ml (1½ pints) tropical fruit juice or drink
Poached Kumquats (see page 115), to serve

1 Put the lemon juice into a large bowl and sprinkle over the gelatine. Leave to stand for 5 minutes or until it is sponge-like in texture. Place over a pan of gently simmering water and heat gently until the mixture clears. Stir in the tropical fruit juice.
2 Rinse out six 200 ml (7 fl oz) jelly moulds or one 1.1 litre (2 pint) mould with cold water but do not dry. Pour in the fruit liquid, cover and refrigerate for at least 5 hours until set.
3 To serve, dip the whole moulds very quickly in hot water, pour off any water that has gathered on the top of the jelly, then invert on to a serving plate and shake the mould hard. Carefully lift off the mould. Serve with Poached Kumquats.

NOT SUITABLE FOR FREEZING
70 Calories per serving

BLACKBERRY CHEESECAKES

Preparation time: 10 minutes, plus chilling
Cooking time: 20 minutes

SERVES 6

25 g (1 oz) wholemeal breadcrumbs
25 g (1 oz) rolled oats
25 g (1 oz) wholemeal flour
40 g (1½ oz) ground almonds
2.5 ml (½ tsp) almond essence
40 g (1½ oz) butter or margarine, melted
250 g (9 oz) ricotta cheese
250 g (9 oz) low-fat set bio yogurt
15 ml (1 tbsp) low-calorie sweetener
225 g (8 oz) blackberries
icing sugar for dusting

1 Mix together the breadcrumbs, oats, flour, almonds, almond essence and melted butter or margarine. Divide the mixture among six 9 cm (3½ inch) loose-base flan tins or transfer it to one shallow, ovenproof dish, and press the mixture down to make a firm base. Bake at 190°C (375°F) mark 5 for 10–15 minutes. Leave to cool.
2 Place the ricotta, yogurt and sweetener in a food processor or blender and process for 15–20 seconds or until well combined. Spoon the mixture on top of the bases and refrigerate for about 2 hours or until set.
3 Remove from the flan tins, if using, top with the blackberries and dust with a little icing sugar. Serve immediately. (If making the cheesecake in just one dish, you will have to spoon it straight from the dish to serve).

NOT SUITABLE FOR FREEZING
225 Calories per serving

FRESH FRUIT JELLY

RUBY ORANGE AND MANDARIN TERRINE

Preparation time: 15 minutes, plus chilling
Cooking time: 5 minutes

SERVES 6

If you can't find ruby oranges or juice, use ordinary orange juice coloured with about 15 ml (1 tbsp) sieved raspberry purée.

600 ml (1 pint) freshly squeezed ruby orange juice
600 ml (1 pint) freshly squeezed mandarin or orange juice
30 ml (2 tbsp) caster sugar
30 ml (2 tbsp) powdered gelatine
30 ml (2 tbsp) chopped fresh mint
fresh raspberries and orange segments, to decorate

1 Rinse out a 1.1 litre (2 pint) terrine or mould with cold water, but do not dry. Spoon 90 ml (6 tbsp) ruby orange juice into a small bowl, add 15 ml (1 tbsp) caster sugar and sprinkle 15 ml (1 tbsp) gelatine over the top. Repeat with the mandarin juice and remaining sugar and gelatine in a separate bowl. Leave both to soak for 5–10 minutes or until needed.
2 Heat the ruby orange juice mixture very gently over a saucepan of gently simmering water until the sugar and gelatine have dissolved: do not boil. Stir in the remaining ruby orange juice, then pour into the terrine or mould. Refrigerate for 2 hours or until set.
3 Heat the mandarin juice mixture very gently over a saucepan of gently simmering water until the sugar and gelatine have dissolved. Stir in the remaining mandarin juice and the mint.
4 Gently scratch the surface of the ruby orange jelly with a fork. Pour the mandarin and mint jelly into the terrine and return to the refrigerator for about 2 hours, or overnight, until set. (The mint rises to the surface to form a layer at the top)
5 To serve, dip the terrine briefly into warm water and turn out on to a serving plate. Use a warmed serrated knife to cut the terrine into 2.5 cm (1 inch) slices. Place on a serving plate, decorate with raspberries and orange segments and serve.

NOT SUITABLE FOR FREEZING
130 Calories per serving

COOK'S TIP
Wet the serving plate before turning out the terrine. This enables you to reposition the terrine.

WARM NUTMEG CUSTARDS

Preparation time: 10 minutes
Cooking time: 45 minutes

SERVES 6

45 ml (3 tbsp) caster sugar
450 ml (¾ pint) skimmed milk
4 eggs
1.25 ml (¼ tsp) grated nutmeg
75 ml (5 tbsp) very low-fat fromage frais
freshly grated nutmeg, to serve

1 Place the sugar and milk in a saucepan and heat gently until the sugar dissolves. Leave to cool slightly.
2 Whisk together the eggs, nutmeg, milk mixture and fromage frais. Strain into six 150 ml (¼ pint) ramekin dishes.
3 Stand the dishes in a roasting tin with enough warm water to come halfway up their sides. Cover the whole tin with foil.
4 Bake at 170°C (325°F) mark 3 for about 45 minutes or until just set. Leave to cool for about 20 minutes. Sprinkle with a generous grating of fresh nutmeg and serve warm.

NOT SUITABLE FOR FREEZING
130 Calories per serving

APPLE AND MANGO GRANITA

Preparation time: 10 minutes plus freezing
Cooking time: nil

SERVES 8

1.1 litres (2 pints) unsweetened apple and mango juice
pared rind and strained juice of 2 lemons
175 g (6 oz) caster sugar

1 Place the apple and mango juice, lemon rind and juice and sugar in a saucepan. Heat gently until the sugar dissolves. Bring to the boil and boil for 1 minute, then pour into a bowl and leave to cool.
2 Strain the liquid into a shallow, freezerproof container. Cover and freeze for about 4 hours or until mushy.
3 Turn into a large bowl and whisk until the ice crystals have broken down. Return to the container, cover and freeze until firm.
4 Transfer to the refrigerator about 30 minutes before serving. Roughly crush the ice crystals and serve in tall glasses.

SUITABLE FOR FREEZING
145 Calories per serving

COOKS' TIP
For a creamier ice, stir in 425 g (15 oz) very low-fat natural yogurt with 3 lightly whisked egg whites after the mixture has been whisked in step 3. Freeze again until firm.
Serves 10. 145 Calories per serving.

APPLE MERINGUES

Preparation time: 30 minutes plus chilling
Cooking time: 1 hour

SERVES 6

2 egg whites
125 g (4 oz) caster sugar
350 g (12 oz) tart eating apples, peeled, cored and thinly sliced
15 ml (1 tbsp) granulated artificial sweetener
4 sprigs of fresh mint
150 g (5 oz) Greek-style yogurt
icing sugar, sprigs of fresh mint and apple slices, to decorate

1 Whisk the egg whites until stiff. Add 30 ml (2 tbsp) caster sugar and whisk again until stiff and shiny. Fold in the remaining sugar.
2 Mark twelve 7.5 cm (3 inch) rounds on a sheet of baking parchment. Smooth the meringue mixture into the rounds. Bake at 140°C (275°F) mark 1 for 1 hour or until dried out and crisp. Leave to cool.
3 Place the apples in a saucepan with the artificial sweetener, mint and 30 ml (2 tbsp) water. Cover and cook gently for about 10 minutes or until the apples have softened slightly. Leave to cool then refrigerate for at least 1 hour. Remove the mint sprigs.
4 Sandwich the meringues with the apple and yogurt. Dust with icing sugar, decorate with mint and apple slices and serve.

MERINGUES ONLY SUITABLE FOR FREEZING
135 Calories per serving

APPLE AND FIG STRUDEL

Preparation time: 25 minutes
Cooking time: 30 minutes

SERVES 6

125 g (4 oz) no-soak dried figs, roughly chopped
grated rind and juice of 1 lemon
25 g (1 oz) fresh white breadcrumbs
450 g (1 lb) cooking apples, peeled, cored and thinly sliced
4 sheets of filo pastry, about 125 g (4 oz) total weight
25 g (1 oz) very low-fat spread, melted
5 ml (1 tsp) caster sugar
icing sugar for dusting

1 Place the figs in a large bowl with the lemon rind and juice, breadcrumbs and apples.

2 Lay two pieces of filo pastry side by side on a clean tea towel, overlapping the longest edges by about 5 cm (2 inches). Brush with a little melted low-fat spread. Top with the other two sheets of pastry and brush again.

3 Place the apple mixture along the longest edge and roll up, using the tea towel to help you. Roll on to a non-stick baking sheet, curling it slightly to fit the sheet. Brush with the remaining low-fat spread and sprinkle with the sugar.

4 Bake at 190°C (375°F) mark 5 for 30–35 minutes or until the pastry is golden brown and the apple is quite soft. Cover with foil if necessary to prevent overbrowning. Serve hot, dusted lightly with icing sugar.

SUITABLE FOR FREEZING
160 Calories per serving

LEFT: GLAZED NECTARINE TART (PAGE 122)
RIGHT: APPLE AND FIG STRUDEL

LEMON AND RASPBERRY PUFFS

Preparation time: 15 minutes
Cooking time: 20 minutes

SERVES 6

40 g (1½ oz) very low-fat spread, plus extra for greasing
225 g (8 oz) raspberries
15 g (½ oz) icing sugar
25 g (1 oz) plain flour
200 ml (7 fl oz) skimmed milk
2 eggs, separated
25 g (1 oz) caster sugar
grated rind of 2 lemons
45 ml (3 tbsp) lemon juice
icing sugar for dusting

1 Lightly grease six 150 ml (¼ pint) ramekin dishes. Purée the raspberries and icing sugar in a food processor. Rub through a nylon sieve then divide among the ramekin dishes.
2 Melt the low-fat spread in a saucepan. Add the flour and cook, stirring, for 1 minute. Gradually blend in the milk. Bring to the boil, stirring, and cook for about 1 minute, whisking until smooth. Leave to cool slightly.
3 Beat in the egg yolks, followed by the caster sugar and lemon rind and juice.
4 Whisk the egg whites until stiff but not dry. Using a large metal spoon, beat one small spoonful of egg white into the sauce to lighten it, then carefully fold in the remainder. Spoon the mixture into the prepared dishes and place on a baking sheet.
5 Bake at 190°C (375°F) mark 5 for 15–20 minutes or until lightly set. Dust with icing sugar and serve immediately.

NOT SUITABLE FOR FREEZING
120 Calories per serving

GLAZED NECTARINE TART

Preparation time: 10 minutes
Cooking time: 15 minutes

SERVES 6

175 g (6 oz) puff pastry
550 g (1¼ lb) ripe nectarines or peaches, stoned and sliced
25 g (1 oz) very low-fat spread, melted
30 ml (2 tbsp) apricot jam

1 Thinly roll out the pastry to a 28 cm (11 inch) round. Place on a non-stick baking sheet and prick all over with a fork. Bake at 230°C (450°F) mark 8 for 8–10 minutes or until well browned.
2 Brush the pastry with the low-fat spread and scatter the fruit over, right to the edges of the pastry. Drizzle with the remaining spread and grill for 5 minutes or until the fruit is just tinged with colour. Leave to cool slightly.
3 Place the apricot jam in a saucepan with a little water and heat gently until melted. Brush over the fruit to glaze. Serve warm.

NOT SUITABLE FOR FREEZING
165 Calories per serving

VARIATION
ALMOND PEACH TART
Bake the pastry base for 6–7 minutes or until just golden. Top with 75 g (3 oz) marzipan rolled out as thinly as possible. Return to the oven for about 2 minutes or until the almond paste begins to melt. Top with peaches as above. Grill for 3–4 minutes and serve immediately without glazing. Serve with a little low-fat fromage frais if wished. Serves 6. 200 Calories per serving.

CITRUS-SYRUP SPONGE CAKE

Preparation time: 30 minutes
Cooking time: 40 minutes

SERVES 8–10

white vegetable fat for greasing
150 g (5 oz) plain flour
5 ml (1 tsp) baking powder
200 ml (7 fl oz) orange juice
3 eggs, separated
275 g (10 oz) caster sugar
5 ml (1 tsp) grated lemon rind
15 ml (3 tsp) grated orange rind
15 ml (1 tbsp) lemon juice
orange slices and blueberries, to serve

1 Grease and base-line a 24 cm (9½ inch) deep, loose-base cake tin. Sift together the flour and baking powder. Put 100 ml (4 fl oz) orange juice in a saucepan and heat gently.
2 Place the egg yolks, 175 g (6 oz) sugar and 30 ml (2 tbsp) hot water in a large bowl and beat with an electric whisk until the mixture has doubled in volume and leaves a trail on the surface.
3 With the whisk at slow speed, gradually add the hot orange juice along with the lemon rind and 10 ml (2 tsp) orange rind. Gradually increase the speed and continue to whisk for 5 minutes.
4 Carefully fold in the flour and baking powder. Whisk the egg whites until they form soft peaks, then carefully fold in.
5 Pour the mixture into the cake tin and bake at 180°C (350°F) mark 4 for 30–35 minutes. Cool the cake for 5 minutes before turning out.
6 To make the syrup, combine the remaining sugar, orange juice, orange rind and the lemon juice in a small saucepan. Boil for 1 minute. Remove from the heat and allow to cool for 5 minutes.
7 Place the cake on a wire rack over a plate. Pierce all over with a skewer, drizzle with half the syrup and leave for 10 minutes. Mix the orange slices and blueberries with the remaining syrup. Serve the cake warm or cold, with the fruit and syrup mixture.

NOT SUITABLE FOR FREEZING
200–250 Calories per serving

GINGER PLUMS

Preparation time: 10 minutes
Cooking time: 40 minutes

SERVES 6

450 g (1 lb) plums, halved and stoned
75 g (3 oz) caster sugar
3 eggs
300 ml (½ pint) semi-skimmed milk
grated rind of ½ lemon
5 ml (1 tsp) ground ginger
5 ml (1 tsp) vanilla essence
45 ml (3 tbsp) runny honey

1 Arrange the plums, cut-side down, in a round, shallow 1.1 litre (2 pint) ovenproof dish. Sprinkle with 30 ml (2 tbsp) of the sugar.
2 Whisk the eggs with all the remaining ingredients except the honey to make a smooth custard. Pour over the fruit.
3 Place the dish in a roasting tin filled with enough hot water to reach halfway up the side of the dish. Cook at 150°C (300°F) mark 2 for 40 minutes or until just set. Meanwhile, warm the honey in a small saucepan. Serve the plums immediately, drizzled with the warmed honey.

NOT SUITABLE FOR FREEZING
165 Calories per serving

OVERLEAF: APPLE MERINGUES (PAGE 119)

INDEX

If you have enjoyed *Best of Good Housekeeping Light & Easy*, you may be interested to know that among a wide range of Good Housekeeping publications the following books are also available:

Good Housekeeping Best Dinner Parties (£10.99)

Good Housekeeping Best Summer Food & Barbecues (£10.99)

Good Housekeeping Best 30-Minute Recipes (£10.99)

Good Housekeeping Cookery Club Healthy Eating (£4.99)

These can be found in all good bookshops or call the credit card hotline on 01279 427203 (postage and packing are free)